D0397507

YOU'RE NEXT

GREG STIER

YOU'RE NEXT

Outrageous stories from my life
that could change yours

GREG STIER

Tyndale House Publishers, Inc.,
Carol Stream, Illinois

A Focus on the Family book published by
Tyndale House Publishers, Inc., Carol Stream, Illinois 60188

TYNDALE and Tyndale's quill logo are registered trademarks of Tyndale House
Publishers, Inc.

Editor: Marianne Hering
Cover design: Mark Lane
Cover and author photo: Wayne Armstrong

Library of Congress Cataloging-in-Publication Data
Stier, Greg.
  You're next : outrageous stories from my life that could change yours / by Greg
Stier.
       p. cm.
  "A Focus on the Family book."
  Includes bibliographical references.
  ISBN-13: 978-1-58997-371-8
  ISBN-10: 1-58997-371-2
  1. Stier, Greg. 2. Christian biography. 3. Christian life. I. Title.
  BR1725.S75A3 2007
  277.3'0825092—dc22
  [B]
                                                    2007007360

Printed in the United States of America
3 4 5 6 7 8 9 / 12 11 10 09 08

To Kailey Autumn Stier—
Although you're too young to read these words, you're not too
young to know that your daddy loves you. My prayer is that,
when it comes to knowing and serving Jesus, you're next.

Contents

Acknowledgments ix

Chapter 0   Outrageous Living
             (Why I'm Writing This Book) 1
Chapter 1   Death Encounter #1: War of the Womb 7
Chapter 2   Ma, the Bat, and the Purpose of Life 17
Chapter 3   Shattered Glass, Slit Wrists, and Sin 26
Chapter 4   Death Encounter #2: Poisoned 33
Chapter 5   Demon Dogs Are After Me 45
Chapter 6   Jack and Jesus 54
Chapter 7   Hell Made Me Pee My Pants 64
Chapter 8   Bob and God 75
Chapter 9   Let Jesus into Your What? 84
Chapter 10   Bullets, Bibles, and the 'Burbs 93
Chapter 11   Death Encounter #3: Butterscotch Candy . . . 102
Chapter 12   Adam, Eve, and the Missing Link 111
Chapter 13   Who's Your Daddy? 118
Chapter 14   Yankee's Weird, Wild, and Wonderful
             Church 126
Chapter 15 $50 Worth of Pennies Buys a Lot 135
Chapter 16   Report Cards on Judgment Day 147
Chapter 17   The Cloud that Haunts Me Still 155
Chapter 18   A Whole Lot of Shaking Going On 162
Chapter 19   The Phone Call from Hell 169
Chapter 20   Salvation and Seizures 179
Chapter 21   Me, Art, and Billy 187

Chapter 22   Mace in My Face 196

Chapter 23   Turnaround and Fadeaway 205

Chapter 24   "Heaven Is Nonsmoking, Ma!" 215

Chapter 25   Death Encounter #4: Massive Heart Attack . . . 224

Chapter 26   One Rogue Uncle 233

Chapter 27   Puppy Love, Broken Hearts, and the Trinity . . . 243

Chapter 28   Run! Run! Granny's Got a Gun! 253

Chapter 29   "You Stinker!" 263

Chapter 30   Choose to Lose 272

The Big Q Chart 284

Notes 285

Acknowledgments

Special thanks go out to Jane Dratz (of Dare 2 Share) and Marianne Hering (of Focus on the Family). Without your editing skills, patience, and prayers this book would have never been pulled off! Thank you for the insights, honest feedback, and ongoing encouragement!

I also want to thank my former theology professor and the original president of Dare 2 Share Ministries, Jonathan Smith. Your passion for truth, God's Word, and solid theology is contagious. From the time I took my first theology class with you 20 years ago I have been fully "infected" with that same passion.

Thank you to the anonymous pastor who left an original eight-volume set of Lewis Sperry Chafer's *Systematic Theology* at my house when I was 15 years old. Whoever you are and for whatever reason you were prompted to do that, just know it gave me my first taste of the importance of knowing, feeling, and living the great doctrines of God's Word.

Finally, I want to thank all of the Dare 2 Share staff, board members, donors, and prayer warriors. Your dedication to and for the mission of "energizing and equipping a generation to know, live, share, and own their faith in Jesus" has given me the fuel to keep pushing, provoking, and proclaiming. I love you all!

Outrageous Living (Why I'm Writing This Book)

A s I type these words, I'm at the hospital. My mom is just a few feet away from me, hanging on to life by a thin thread, the same thin thread she has walked like a tightrope her entire life. This time the only net that will catch her is the loving embrace of Jesus. Her labored breathing is interrupted by the occasional horrible, hacking smoker's cough. The nurses tell me she is about to slip into a coma. Lung cancer will be the death of her . . . soon.

Ma is hard to describe. She is a strange combination of tough and tender, rage and compassion, strength and beauty. Many would say she is the nicest, most authentic person they ever met. Others are scared to death of her. If you are a good person, she will give you the shirt off her back. If you are mean, selfish, or condescending, you might want to duck.

For the last few weeks I've been sleeping in her hospital room on the hospice floor. Sleeping may be an overstatement. Between the nurses administering "pain-management" drugs and my mom's continual outbursts that range from confused—"Where am I?"—to delusional—"The lady is on fire, Greg! Put her out!"—to hopeful—

"I can't wait to get to heaven!"—to sad—"Why won't God just let me die?"—sleep is more of a hope than a reality.

Walking the hospital hallways is driving me crazy. Sitting here trying to have conversations with my near-comatose mom is breaking my heart. I have to write or I am going to burst. Reading or writing words has always been cathartic for me. The expression of emotions and ideas through sentences and paragraphs has brought me comfort ever since I was a child.

I'm writing this book in part to release my emotions as I tell you stories from life before I left my teenage years. These stories focus on the truths I learned from the weird and sometimes dangerous events that happened to me—events that transformed the way I thought about life and God. I believe these truths can change you as well by helping you grow deeper in your walk with God. As you understand more and more about who God is, you'll be transformed by His power at work in you and through you. As God draws you into relationship with Him and changes you, He will use you to change your world.

Through this book, I hope that you will also see how God is at work in life's everyday circumstances and how He is revealing Himself to you. No matter how tough or easy your life has been, you can see God is at work in your story—just as He was in mine—and He's using your experiences to shape and mold you and draw you toward Himself.

As you read some of these outrageous stories from my life, you'll see that I don't come from a churchgoing, pew-sitting, hymn-singing family. I come from a family filled with bodybuilders, brawlers, and storytellers. In many ways my family members are more like a tribal people from some distant continent who lived to do battle during the day and show battle scars around the campfire at night.

The stories that you are about to read in this book, as best as I can determine, are true. Most of these stories I was directly involved in; the other ones, which are usually about a family member or took place when I was too young to remember, have been confirmed and reconfirmed by family members and with outside witnesses.

Everyone who told me about Ma (not Mom or Mother but "Ma") swore the stories were true. I heard them from too many people to doubt they happened. Once when my mom was a teenager, some girl gang member pulled a knife on her in a movie theater. Ma threw her over the balcony. When she was in high school she was a member of a girl's gang called "The Curls." She kept a straight razor hidden in her hair and wasn't afraid to use it. She would fight guys two at a time without thinking or blinking. The stories of her violent outbursts go on and on and on. Some are too gruesome to put in this book.

I witnessed a few of her outbursts. Something in her past had hurt her deeply, and her rage was always lurking in the shadows like a wounded grizzly ready to attack. Some soul trigger hidden deep inside her heart would be squeezed, and she would morph before our very eyes into a tornado of fury. This volcanic rage would usually end up badly for the offending person. But I know that her flailing fists were taking swings at the pain in her soul more than the person in front of her.

And now she is lying in a hospital bed at my side, on the brink of death. My once strong mom is a shadow of the person she was just a few years ago. It is breaking my heart.

When my mom was more alert a few weeks ago, we walked down memory lane for hours, for days. We talked about life growing up in inner-city Denver. We talked about the fights we witnessed over the years. We talked about how Jesus changed everything.

She loved that I was using the story of our family to communicate biblical truth to teenagers. She loved the fact that, by God's grace, I was rescued from the path she had taken as a young person. She was proud that I was a preacher and that I was working to equip teenagers to know, live, and share their faith in Jesus. The last time Ma came to a Dare 2 Share conference I led, she stood in the back of an arena full of thousands of teens and beamed with excitement because teenagers were being called to choose the narrow path that leads to eternal life rather than the highway to destruction that she had picked as a teenager.

Why am I writing this book? Because I've seen what the power of Jesus can do in transforming a life and an entire family. Because I long to see an army of Jesus-loving teens rise up and transform this planet for God. Because Ma wanted me to.

As I sit watching my mom die, I am reminded of the wild life she had on this side of eternity, the same kind of craziness that most of my entire family has experienced on some level. I am reminded of how God used the insane things that happened to me to turn me into a "Jesus freak" before my 18th birthday. My prayer is that God will use this book, the stories in it, and especially the truths in it to turn you into a Jesus-loving superfanatic, too.

I hope you'll be next.

P.S. Ma died at 7:25 A.M. What an outrageous life she lived.

The Story Behind the Stories

Each chapter in *You're Next* tells one story from my life. Some of these stories are pretty intense. I come from a very violent background. Some of these stories are funny. But all of these true stories taught me a lesson about the Christianity that I now fully embrace.

So here's how it goes. I did my best to make these stories chronological, so this book starts with my early life and finishes with my senior year of high school. Each chapter seeks to answer a question about Christianity, which I call **The Big Q**. After addressing The Big Q, each chapter will ask the question **So What?** In this section I will help you think through why this particular truth of Christianity is important and what difference it should make in your life.

In addition to The Big Q and So What? each chapter also includes four other features. (1) **Blast from the Past**: A quote, poem, or creed from the past that explains the answer to The Big Q in a brief, biblical, and memorable way. (2) **Go Figure!** A Bible passage and questions that deal with The Big Q, helping you understand and apply the passage to your life. (3) **Insane Brain Strain**: A hard aspect about the truth; it is designed to provoke your mind a bit and get the neurons firing. (4) **You're Next!** A kind of journal-meets-action-plan section where you can write out your thoughts, prayers, and feelings about how you are choosing to make a change in your life based on that chapter's truth.

This book contains the story of my life, but ultimately it's not about me. It's a theology book that explains the core truths of Christianity in a relevant and fun way. But it's not just a theology book. The reason it's called *You're Next* is because I want this book to impact your own life story. As you read how God forged and formed my theology in real life situations, my passionate prayer is that you will allow God to do the same in you and through you. The Word of God is just as relevant today as when the words were penned thousands of years ago. If you let the truth from Scripture help to write your story, you will be in for the thrill ride of your life with Jesus by your side all the way.

Take it from a guy who's lived a pretty outrageous life himself.

Cute as a baby . . . but I grew out of it!

CHAPTER 1

Death Encounter #1: War of the Womb

We never talked about it. Not once in 38 years. But I knew. She had a secret, and she didn't want me to find out about it. It hung over my mom like a dark cloud. What was it? I'll tell you in a bit. But before I do, there is something you need to know.

I love my mom, and she loved my brother, Doug, and me with all of her heart. She raised us the best she knew how, but she worried. Almost every night she wept and begged us not to turn out like her.

As I grew from a child to a teenager, confusion and questions filled my heart and my head. But there was one thing I was never confused about, one truth that I never questioned: My mom loved me.

So I couldn't understand the cloud over Ma. I didn't know what caused the darkness until one day, out of the blue, my grandma told me. What was this dark secret that mom had worked so hard to keep? That she had come dangerously close to having an abortion, that she had almost killed me.

Now, some who knew my mom are probably shocked by this, and some may deny it. But I know that what my grandmother told me that fateful day was completely true. Although it was painful to hear, it actually helped me understand why my mom felt so guilty all the time. It helped me understand why for so long she had been resistant to put her faith in Jesus. She thought she was too sinful to save.

Though we never spoke of it, I can speculate at her possible motives for considering an abortion. At the time I guess Ma didn't think that Grandma and Grandpa, her strict Baptist parents, would understand that their black sheep daughter had gotten pregnant, this time out of wedlock. I'm sure she was terrified they would find out that their rebellious daughter had messed up and threatened to break their hearts again. Ma couldn't stomach the thought of seeing another look of disappointment in her parents' eyes.

Besides, she already had a son from one of her past marriages. He was the single bright spot in her life, even though little Doug had his set of unique challenges. Not only did he have epilepsy and some learning disabilities, but there were other problems. Being raised by a single mom on a single income without government assistance in one of the highest crime-rate areas in inner-city Denver, Doug had the odds stacked against him. The last thing Ma needed was another kid. She didn't want to bring another child into her world, a world of pain, a world of violence, a world of guilt.

Additionally, the guy who was the "father" wasn't going to take any financial responsibility. As soon as he found out Ma was pregnant he moved two thousand miles away . . . literally. So why not abort? Maybe she could abort a little of her shame in the process.

There was only one problem for her: It was 1965, and abortion was still illegal in the United States. This meant that she had to find somebody, somewhere, who would do an illegal abortion. So, under the pretense of visiting relatives, she drove east toward Boston, where she planned to rid herself of the shame she felt in her womb and her soul. God's grace, second thoughts, and a phone call from her parents (who found out what she was up to) rescued me from a shady surgeon's instruments of death.

Even though she chose the right path, the guilt still haunted her. Every time she looked at me, she was reminded that she had almost ended my life. Throughout my elementary and junior high school years I didn't understand this bittersweet look in Ma's eyes. But Grandma's inside information, as painful as it was, helped me understand the unrelenting guilt in my mother's soul. It also helped me understand the pent-up anger that was always ready to explode from within her.

I had always had a lot of confusion about the whole dad thing. I thought that my brother and I had the same father. But Doug's dad never wanted to talk to me. If I answered the phone when he called, he would just say, "Put your brother on the line." I thought he just hated me.

But he wasn't my dad; he was Doug's. I was somewhere around 12 years old when I found out that my real dad had left town before I was ever born. This news rocked my world. It shocked me, a vulnerable seventh-grader struggling with self-identity.

So what got me through? The answer is simple: God.

In one of her more lucid moments as my mom lay waiting to die, we were talking about my childhood and our struggles in the tough part of town. Then she asked me a question I'll never forget. "Do you remember what you used to say to kids who made fun of you for not having a dad?"

"No, Ma," I said. "I don't remember."

"You used to say, 'God's my Daddy.' "

When it comes to the question of who God is and what He is like, you need to understand I take this question personally. To me, God is the only Father I've ever had. He is my role model, mentor, and hero. He is my Daddy.

If you have put your faith and trust in Jesus as your only hope of going to heaven, then God is your Daddy, too. Jesus said, "I am the way and the truth and the life. No one comes to the Father except through me. If you really knew me, you would know my Father as well. From now on, you do know him and have seen him" (John 14:6-7).

Although I don't know a lot about my earthly father, I know a lot about my heavenly one. From the time I was little I've scoured His love letters to me—the Bible. I've poured out my heart to Him through prayer. I've thought about Him in the daytime and dreamed of Him at night. He has been the anchor for my soul, my comforter in painful times, my closest friend and confidant, my loving master, my loving God, my gracious Savior.

Do you know Him? Do you know what He is like?

The Big Q: Who is God, and what is He like?

Since the beginning of humankind, people have attempted to answer this question, many to no avail.

How do we define the indefinable? How do we use our limited minds to describe a limitless subject? We don't. We let the indefinable and indescribable define and describe Himself.

So where does God define and describe Himself? In the second book of the Bible:

> Moses said to God, "Suppose I go to the Israelites and say to
> them, 'The God of your fathers has sent me to you,' and they ask
> me, 'What is his name?' Then what shall I tell them?"
>
> God said to Moses, "I AM WHO I AM. This is what you are to
> say to the Israelites: 'I AM has sent me to you.' "
>
> God also said to Moses, "Say to the Israelites, 'The LORD,
> the God of your fathers—the God of Abraham, the God of Isaac

and the God of Jacob—has sent me to you.' This is my name forever, the name by which I am to be remembered from generation to generation." (Exodus 3:13-15)

In this passage, God is trying to talk Moses into confronting Pharaoh and rescuing the Israelites from the tyranny of the Egyptians. Moses is freaking—and not in the positive "Jesus freak" sense. The real truth is that Moses is afraid. He does not want to be the deliverer of the Israelites.

Right in the middle of his laundry list of excuses he basically asks God, "Hey, what do I say if they want to know your name?"

God's answer is direct and powerful: "I AM WHO I AM. This is what you are to say to the Israelites: 'I AM has sent me to you.' "

Now this may seem like a weird thing to say. Why would anybody have the name "I AM," especially God?

One reason was to emphasize to Moses and the Israelites (and to us) that there was only one true God. In a culture where many gods were worshiped, God was teaching Moses the reality that there is only one true God.

> **BLAST FROM THE PAST**
>
> We believe in one God the Father Almighty, Maker of heaven and earth, and of all things visible and invisible.[1]
>
> —NICENE CREED, 4TH CENTURY

The truth that there is only one God isn't the truth that blew me away when I was a child. The truth that rattled my cage and transformed my thinking was the reality that God *is*. Before I was born, God *is*. Although I was confused about who I was, God has never been perplexed about who He is.

He is the eternally self-existent one. What does that mean? It means that He doesn't need food, air, shelter, or companionship. He exists with or without us. He has always been and will always be here. Before you or I were ever born, He is.

Let's take a look at what God is:

He is there. Smart guys (aka *theologians*) call this omnipresence. Simply put this means that God is everywhere all the time. He is ever-present. King David put it this way:

Where can I go from your Spirit?

Where can I flee from your presence?

If I go up to the heavens, you are there;

if I make my bed in the depths, you are there.

If I rise on the wings of the dawn,

if I settle on the far side of the sea,

even there your hand will guide me,

your right hand will hold me fast. (Psalm 139:7-10)

To put it straight up, you can't get away from God. You can run, but you can't hide. But it also means (and this is the part that helped me turn into a fanatic for Jesus) that He is always there to hold me up when I feel like giving up. While my earthly dad was gone before I was born, my heavenly Dad would never let me out of His sight. Why? Because He is there.

Not only is He there, . . .

He is holy. The word *holy* means that He is set apart, pure, totally unique, and different. God is so pure that He will blow your mind. He is set apart from sin and set apart to perfection, to righteousness (think of rightness on steroids), to sheer purity.

Have you ever seen a label on a bottle, can, or container that read, "100 percent pure"? Well, it's a lie. I guarantee that if you look closely enough, you'll find some microbes or molecules that shouldn't be in it.

The only thing in this universe that you could truly put the 100 percent pure label on is God Himself. He is 100 percent pure, without any sin or imperfection.

What significance does this have for you as a young person? The same it had for me. If God is holy, we should aspire to be holy too, seeing as how this holy God is our Daddy. Maybe that's why He tells us in 1 Peter 1:14-16, "As obedient children, do not conform to the evil desires you had when you lived in ignorance. But just as he who called you is holy, so be holy in all you do; for it is written: **'Be holy, because I am holy.' "**

Go Figure!

Open your Bible, ask God for help to understand, and read Romans 8:12-17. Answer these questions:

1. What does it look like when we live according to the "sinful nature"?

   _____

   _____

   _____

2. What are some ways we can "put to death the misdeeds of the body"?

   _____

   _____

   _____

3. How does it feel to be one of "God's children"?

   _____

   _____

   _____

4. The word *Abba* used in this passage means "Daddy." Do you consider God your "Daddy"? Why or why not?

_____

_____

_____

5. How does this passage show that God is both holy and our Father?

_____

_____

_____

We are called to be holy as He is holy! That has myspace.com, movie, dating, masturbation, Internet, and music-choice implications!

So why try? Because He is!

He is there. He is watching. He is holy.

But He is so much more!

- **He is all-powerful!** "Is anything too hard for the LORD?" (Genesis 18:14)

- **He is all-knowing!** "Oh, the depth of the riches of the wisdom and knowledge of God! How unsearchable his judgments, and his paths beyond tracing out!" (Romans 11:33)

- **He is all-loving!** "Dear friends, let us love one another, for love comes from God. Everyone who loves has been born of God and knows God. Whoever does not love does not know God, because God is love." (1 John 4:7-8)

- **He is eternal!** " 'I am the Alpha and the Omega,' says the Lord God, 'who is, and who was, and who is to come, the Almighty.' " (Revelation 1:8)

The list goes on and on and on. Suffice it to say that God is bigger, more awesome, more amazing, and more shocking than any puny thing you or I have ever seen on this planet.

He is bigger than we are. He is the Creator of all that we will ever see (Genesis 1:1). He holds everything together by His power (Colossians 1:17). He is the supreme ruler of the universe (Revelation 19), yet He loves us enough to die for us (John 3:16).

INSANE BRAIN STRAIN

God has no beginning. How can that be? If He is, then not only will He always be here, but He has always been here. Some have described His existence as a ring, no beginning and no end, just a continuous circle of existence. But even with this illustration to help, the concept still blows my mind. Does it blow yours?

So What?

The fact that there is an all-powerful God who is perfect and in complete control of the universe changes everything! Think about it—you can relax in His guidance, and you can know that even when things don't seem to make sense, God will work it all out in the end. The coolest thing is that no matter what kind of relationship you have with your earthly father, you will always have a perfect and powerful heavenly Father who will never let you down. And because God is holy, this should motivate you to be like your Daddy and live a life pleasing to Him!

Weird, wild, and a reason to worship.

He is, when we are not, when our dads are not, when life is not.

It's enough to turn you into a Jesus freak. Ma would have been proud.

YOU'RE NEXT!

God is my Daddy! He is your Daddy too! And He is! He is there. He is holy. He is loving, eternal, merciful, and more! Let "I am" know what you are most thankful about when it comes to who He is! I already told you mine. You're next!

Dear God,

_____

_____

_____

_____

_____

_____

_____

_____

_____

_____

_____

_____

_____

✳ ✳ ✳

For more info on **The Big Q: Who is God, and what is He like?** visit www.dare2share.org/soulfuel/archives and check out *Soul Fuel* question #1.

CHAPTER 2

Ma, the Bat, and the Purpose of Life

When I was five years old, I had an experience that left a vivid, dramatic, and traumatic memory. My mom had married a guy named Paul a few months earlier, and one day, he up and left.

Paul left no note. He didn't give any indication that he was leaving or why. But when Ma came home from work that day, he and his bags were gone.

Ma was steamed. What kind of man would just leave without even an explanation? The more she thought about it, the angrier she got. I remember her random outbursts: "Paul, that jerk! If I ever get a hold of him I'll . . ." She would go on to describe in vivid detail the pain she planned on inflicting on her AWOL husband. Although I was little, I knew that Paul had better steer clear of Ma.

He didn't.

One Saturday a few weeks later Paul pulled up to our little rental house in a brand-new shiny car. While he was gone on his marriage sabbatical (or whatever it was), he decided he needed to roll in some new wheels. I was playing on the porch with a plastic bat and some balls when Paul cruised to a stop in front of our place.

At first I didn't know who it was. I squinted through the glare of the windows to see Paul in the driver's seat. He didn't get out. He was just sitting there. Looking back now, I'm sure he was asking himself whether he should have come back. He was probably thinking something like this: *It's been a few weeks, so I'm sure that Shirley has calmed down. Should I go in? Her temper can't be as bad as I've heard from her friends. I've never seen her do anything bad. I'm sure this won't turn physical. And besides, she's just a woman, and I'm a man.*

As soon as I recognized Paul, I ran inside and yelled, "Ma—one of my daddies is here."

Ma looked out the window and started screaming, "It's Paul, that jerk! Where's the baseball bat?" I had been playing with my plastic bat, so I offered mine. She declined. She was looking for Old Faithful, the real wooden bat we kept behind the door in case of intruders.

She grabbed Old Faithful and ran out the door. She sprinted past me and straight to Paul's brand-new car. In one fell swoop she smashed the front windshield. She proceeded to break every window on that car while screaming a steady flow of obscenities, taunting Paul to get out. But he didn't. He sat stunned behind the wheel of his car. I think he was contemplating whether he should drive away or try to stop her from further damage. He decided to get out of the car and try to stop her.

Bad idea.

Ma took the bat and inflicted the worst beating I've ever seen on anyone by anyone. He just kept screaming, trying to get away from my mom's relentless swing. Covered in blood, he finally stumbled to his shattered and dented brand-new car and drove away, never to be seen again.

After Paul drove off into oblivion and my mom began to walk back up the sidewalk to our house with that splintered bat, which was now covered in blood, I remember thinking, *I will never disobey Ma again!*

Watching this kind of real-life violence was pretty traumatic for me at the time. Seeing that kind of violence at such a young age shook my sense of safety and security. It shook up my image of my mom and blew apart my innocent, childlike sense of the world and my place it in. It made me grow up faster than most kids and pushed me into a mode of introspection. From the time I was a young child, I wondered who I was and what the purpose of life was. It had to be something different from what I had witnessed in my mom's life.

The Big Q: Who am I, where did I come from, and what is my purpose?

This question plagued me as a five-year-old. I didn't have a sense of self or where I had come from because I didn't know anything about my real dad. Although I did not understand the gospel yet, I had a strong sense of God's presence in my life. I went to church with my grandparents to find out more about this God.

Over the following years I discovered more and more about Him. The more I discovered about who He is, the more I found out about who I was. Three years later, when I finally understood the gospel, it gave me a strong sense of identity. I discovered where I came from and what I was here for.

So what is the answer to The Big Q?

I am a child of God, created to be in fellowship with Him, designed to bring Him glory! Ephesians 2:10 puts it this way: "For we are God's workmanship, created in Christ Jesus to do good works, which God prepared in advance for us to do."

We are a result of God's hard work. He created us physically when we were conceived in our mother's womb. He transformed us spiritually when we put our faith and trust in Jesus for the very first time.

Why did He create us and save us? So that we might do good works that would bring God honor and glory!

 INSANE BRAIN STRAIN

If our purpose is to bring glory to God, then why do we spend so much of our time running from what we were made for?

Every day you and I have the opportunity to do good works. We can love those around us by listening to them, doing acts of kindness that will brighten their day, sharing with them the good news of Jesus in our words and our actions.

Our purpose is to bring maximum glory to God. This attitude should be in everything we do. The good works we do are an expression of the glory that we want to bring to God. Maybe that's why Jesus said, "Let your light shine before men, that they may see your good deeds and praise your Father in heaven" (Matthew 5:16).

BLAST FROM THE PAST

Man's chief end is to glorify God, and to enjoy him forever.[1]

—WESTMINSTER CATECHISM, 17TH CENTURY

What is our purpose? To bring glory to God in our good deeds!

Where did we come from? From God! David put it this way in Psalm 139:13-14: "For you created my inmost being; you knit me together in my mother's womb. I praise you because I am fearfully and wonderfully made; your works are wonderful, I know that full well."

You are not the result of random chance. If God created us, then what does Scripture have to say about all the creation and evolution debate? (More on that later!) You were designed by the hand of God in your mother's womb. He knit you together and handcrafted you to be the masterpiece that you are. Your "defects" make you unique and cause you to trust in God more so that He can make your inner character a masterpiece as well.

Go Figure!

Open your Bible, ask God for help to understand, and read 1 Samuel 17:4-11 and 32-50. Answer these questions:

1. Why was David so bold when all the others were afraid?

   _____

   _____

   _____

2. Do you think David had a sense of who he was? Why or why not?

   _____

   _____

   _____

3. How can knowing who you are and why you are here give you confidence?

   _____

   _____

   _____

4. What are the "giants" you are facing right now?

   _____

   _____

   _____

5. How can knowing that God created you and calls you to honor Him help you defeat those giants?

_____

_____

_____

_____

Who are we? We are children of God, adopted into His family, saved from sin, and heirs to His throne. Check out Galatians 4:4-7:

> But when the time had fully come, God sent his Son, born of a woman, born under law, to redeem those under law, that we might receive the full rights of sons. Because you are sons, God sent the Spirit of his Son into our hearts, the Spirit who calls out, "*Abba*, Father." So you are no longer a slave, but a son; and since you are a son, God has made you also an heir.

Before we put our faith and trust in Jesus as the forgiver of our sins, we stood guilty in the courtroom of God as complete and absolute sinners. But when we believed in Jesus, the payment for our sin was paid in full through the death of Jesus. As a result, God has adopted us as His children. In that sense Jesus is our brother, not through blood, but through adoption. We are coheirs with Jesus! That's why one day we will rule and reign at His side in the coming kingdom! That's why we can cry out to God as our Daddy in prayer and He will listen. He always listens to the prayers of His children who seek to follow Him in obedience.

So What?

As you begin to realize the awesome truth of what your purpose in life is, you will begin to feel incredibly loved and totally motivated. Think about it . . . you have been handcrafted by the God who made the universe—and now you have a chance to put the weight of His name in your corner of the world by doing good deeds! Begin doing things today that will bring glory to God. These can include spending time with a hurting friend, helping out a neighbor with a project, or, best of all, telling people about the God who made them and wants to have a relationship with them!

So the next time you look in the mirror and you don't like what you see, just remember who you are (a child of God), where you came from (God's workmanship), and the purpose you have in this life (to bring glory to God by the good deeds you do). Look in the mirror and smile!

YOU'RE NEXT!

Put your name in the blanks below, then read through the passage several times and meditate/write down thoughts on how this makes you feel.

Psalm 139:1-18

O Lord, you have searched _____
and you know _____ .
You know when I sit and when I rise;
you perceive my thoughts from afar.
You discern my going out and my lying down;
you are familiar with all my ways.
Before a word is on my tongue

you know it completely, O LORD.
You hem me in—behind and before;
you have laid your hand upon me.
Such knowledge is too wonderful for me,
too lofty for me to attain.
Where can _____ go from your Spirit?
Where can _____ flee from your presence?
If I go up to the heavens, you are there;
if I make my bed in the depths, you are there.
If I rise on the wings of the dawn,
if I settle on the far side of the sea,
even there your hand will guide _____ ,
your right hand will hold _____ fast.
If I say, "Surely the darkness will hide me
and the light become night around me,"
even the darkness will not be dark to you;
the night will shine like the day,
for darkness is as light to you.
For you created my inmost being;
you knit me together in my mother's womb.
I praise you because I am fearfully and wonderfully made;
your works are wonderful,
I know that full well.
My frame was not hidden from you
when I was made in the secret place.
When I was woven together in the depths of the earth,
your eyes saw my unformed body.
All the days ordained for _____
were written in your book before one of them came to be.
How precious to me are your thoughts, O God!

How vast is the sum of them!
Were I to count them,
they would outnumber the grains of sand.
When I awake,
I am still with you.

_____

_____

_____

_____

_____

_____

_____

_____

_____

_____

_____

✳ ✳ ✳

For more info on **The Big Q: Who am I, where did I come from, and what is my purpose?** visit www.dare2share.org/soulfuel/archives and check out *Soul Fuel* question #28.

CHAPTER 3

Shattered Glass, Slit Wrists, and Sin

S oon after the baseball bat incident, another episode took place that would scar me for life. This particular day I was at my grandparents' house, playing inside.

One of Grandma's cardinal rules was no running in the house. That's a hard rule for a six-year-old to obey, especially a hyperactive one like me. I had pent-up energy that I had to get out.

With a little plastic gun, I was shooting all of the imaginary bad guys hidden all over my grandparents' old nineteenth-century house. Heading down the hallway to escape the bad guys, I broke the "no running" rule. I was moving straight for a window but planned to make a hard right turn into the kitchen. But at exactly the wrong moment, my grandma yelled, "Greg! No running in the house!" I turned my head to look at her, but my body kept going straight.

With a gigantic crash I penetrated the glass and landed right in the middle of the windowsill. My six-year-old body was dangling in limbo. My head, arms, and upper torso were outside, and my feet, legs, and lower torso were still inside.

I looked down on the porch and saw my brother sitting there. He looked up at me and simply said, "You're in trouble."

I was. My hands and fingers had been shredded by shards of

glass. Worse, my wrists had been slit by the glass. And I was bleeding . . . bad.

My grandma freaked out. She ran around screaming, looking for towels to wrap up my blood-soaked hands. As she did, I didn't cry. I tried to calm her down. Maybe I was in shock or something, but I wasn't really afraid. I was worried for my grandma because I had never seen her hysterical.

After wrapping each of my hands in a towel, she rounded up my brother and her day-care kids and got us in the car. But she was so nervous she couldn't find the keyhole for the ignition. "Grandma," I said to her over and over, "it's going to be okay. Don't worry. Just calm down."

By now I should have been worried. I was losing a lot of blood, and the towels wrapping my hands were red, saturated in blood.

Just then a stranger appeared.

The man knocked on the driver-side window and asked my grandma if she needed some help. She began to cry and said yes, then she frantically explained the situation. "Scoot over, ma'am," the man said. "I'm driving you to the hospital."

This man took us to St. Anthony Central Hospital and helped us in. It took three hours for me to get stitched up and checked out completely. He waited patiently the whole time and then drove us all back to my grandma's house, said good-bye, and left. I never saw him again.

By the way, he was black.

Why is that significant to the story? Because he was the first black person I ever remember seeing. Although I was from the urban part of inner-city Denver, we lived in the Hispanic part of town. The color of his skin was not typical for my neighborhood. He came out of nowhere, sacrificed his time, and very likely saved my life. When I think about that day, I start to wonder how he "happened" to be there to intervene at that particular time and place.

In many ways this caring man is a kind of picture of Christ for me. He saved me from dying, saved me from the consequences of my own sin.

What was my sin? It wasn't jumping through the window—it was running inside and breaking the cardinal rule of Grandma's house.

Did you know that in God's house there is a set of rules called the Ten Commandments? When we break those rules, terrible trouble follows. Our lives are shredded by the shards of sin and broken commandments. We lie waiting to die in a pool of our own disobedience. But then Jesus comes out of nowhere and offers to save us if we simply trust in Him alone.

The Big Q: What is sin, and how does it impact my life and my relationship with others?

The word *sin* simply means "to miss the mark." When we sin, we miss the mark of God's perfect standard. When we lie, we miss the mark. When we steal, we miss the mark. When we brag, we miss the mark. When we lust, cheat, hate, or hurt, we miss the mark.

God puts it this way in Romans 3:23: "For all have sinned and fall short of the glory of God." We all sin. We all fall short. We all miss the mark.

When's the last time you lied, even a little lie? Maybe this came from exaggerating the truth or telling somebody a lie to cover your own mistake. Guess what? That little lie is a big problem with God. When the Bible tells of the New Jerusalem, the crown city of heaven, it says, "Nothing impure will ever enter it, nor will anyone who does what is shameful or **deceitful**, but only those whose names are written in the Lamb's book of life" (Revelation 21:27).

God will never allow any sin or sinner to enter into heaven. Instead, the consequences of our sin are physical death here on earth and eternal death in hell. Check out this verse: "For the wages of sin is death, but the gift of God is eternal life in Christ Jesus our Lord" (Romans 6:23).

You lie, you die. You lust, you die. You hate, you die.

Jesus paid the price for your sin on the cross two thousand years ago, and if you put your faith in Him to forgive your sins completely, then you will see Him in heaven.

> **BLAST FROM THE PAST**
>
> Though Satan instills his poison, and fans the flames of our corrupt desires within us, we are yet not carried by any external force to the commission of sin, but our own flesh entices us, and we willingly yield to its allurements.[1]
>
> —JOHN CALVIN, 16TH CENTURY CHURCH REFORMER

Go Figure!

Open your Bible, ask God for help to read and understand 2 Samuel 11, and answer these questions:

1. David allowed himself to stay in a tempting situation. When do you do the same thing?

   _____

   _____

   _____

2. How did David try to cover his sin? How do you?

   _____

   _____

   _____

3. How could David have avoided the whole situation?

_____

_____

_____

4. How can you avoid tempting situations?

_____

_____

_____

5. What sins have taken hold in your life that need to be eliminated immediately?

_____

_____

_____

The problem is that sin impacts everyone it touches. When we sin, it affects us. My choice to disobey Grandma tore me to shreds . . . literally. But every time we choose to sin, it tears us to shreds. If you lust, you are tearing to shreds your inner character every bit as much as my hands were shredded by that broken glass. Gossip tears apart friendships. Anger tears apart families. Pride tears apart everything.

When we sin, we not only tear apart and do damage to ourselves and to our human relationships, we also tear apart our relationship with God. Psalm 66:18 makes this very clear: "If I had cherished sin in my heart, the LORD would not have listened." This is sobering and scary, because it means that if we are deliberately, defiantly living in sin (breaking the rules of His house) He will not hear our prayers . . . period.

INSANE BRAIN STRAIN

If sin is destructive to our relationship with ourselves, others, and God . . . why do we keep doing it?

As a matter of fact, He will discipline us, and that divine "spanking" or "time out" can hurt. God has a way of getting our attention when we allow sin instead of Him to rule our lives. The Bible explains in Hebrews 12:6 the reason God disciplines us: "The Lord disciplines those he loves, and he punishes everyone he accepts as a son."

Because God loves us, He will not allow sin to rule in our lives. Why? Because sin will shred us like shards of broken glass. Instead of letting sin rule us, He will take out the divine paddle and get our attention, because He loves us. The pain He inflicts is for our own good.

So What?

Now that you know how devastating and damaging sin can be, you should be careful . . . very careful. Sin isn't something you want to play around with like a pet. Sin is the most destructive force in the universe by far, and it is Satan's primary tool to bring misery and ruin to your life. Make a list of tempting situations that oftentimes lead to sinful actions, and figure out how to avoid them. It could be as easy as not watching a certain movie to as difficult as never going on the Internet without someone else in the room. You may also need to end relationships/friendships if they are dragging you into sin. The bottom line is that you must avoid sin like a plague that could kill you—because it is.

So be careful, because you don't want your relationships with God and others to suffer, and you don't want to feel God's spank. Remember . . . no running in the house! Take it from me.

YOU'RE NEXT!

The Bible tells about godly people who are called prophets. One of the jobs prophets had was to bring messages from God, and one of the main messages was "don't sin." If you look through the pages of the Old Testament, you will read about these brave men and women who stood up to kings, cities, and even the entire nation of Israel. They confronted wayward people about the different ways they were sinning against God.

Pretend for a moment that you are a prophet sent by God to confront the sin in your own life. What would be your initial reaction? Pride? Denial? Would you admit to your sin? Argue about it?

Take some time to write down what kind of conversation might take place if that happened.

_____

_____

_____

_____

_____

_____

_____

_____

_____

_____

_____

※ ※ ※

For more info on **The Big Q: What is sin, and how does it impact my life and my relationship with others?** visit www.dare2share.org/soulfuel/archives and check out *Soul Fuel* question #10.

CHAPTER 4

Death Encounter #2: Poisoned

My sheets were drenched in sweat, my body was racked with pain, and my temperature was well past the danger zone for a six-year-old boy. Ma was at a loss. She knew that something was wrong. She had seen fevers before, but this was something different, something worse.

When my body curled up into a tiny ball and my mom couldn't muster the strength to push my knees back from my chest, she rushed me to the emergency room at St. Anthony Central. The doctors put me on a gurney and pushed me to one of the back surgical rooms.

After the examination, the doctors discovered that a lethal poison was coursing through my little body. My appendix had burst, spewing pus and bacteria throughout my system.

For two weeks I lay helpless in the critical-care unit. Tubes, which were jammed down my nose and throat, pumped the poison out of my stomach. My entire body was infected, and the doctors didn't know if I was going to make it.

One day after the surgery, I woke up in a hospital room, afraid. *What are these tubes going down my nose and into my stomach? Where am I? What happened?* Just as fear was about to turn into panic, I turned my head and saw my mom. Her head and hands were on my bed, and she was sleeping. She had spent the night at the hospital waiting for me, praying for me, to wake up. At that moment I knew everything was going to be all right. Ma was there.

As a result of this brush with death, I began to ask questions like "Why would God let a little kid like me go through so much?"

Probably all of us have asked those hard questions: "Why would God allow innocent people to be killed by disease, in a terrorist attack, or in a natural disaster like a tornado, hurricane, tsunami, or earthquake?" But if you really get to the root of the issue, the fundamental question is much bigger and more basic.

The Big Q: Why does God allow evil in this world?

What bad things have happened to you? Maybe your parents got a divorce, or your friend turned on you. Maybe your boyfriend or girlfriend dumped you or you have some kind of disability. Whatever evil has befallen you, just remember this: The answer is wrapped up in the core of human existence. And before we can truly understand why God allows evil in the world, we must first realize how it invaded a good creation.

We must come to grips with the fact that God allowed evil to invade our world from the very beginning of human history. Don't get me wrong; He didn't make it happen, but He definitely let it happen.

Long ago in the Garden of Eden everything was perfect. Adam and Eve, the first man and woman, were in sheer bliss. Here's what happened:

This is the account of the heavens and the earth when they were created.

When the LORD God made the earth and the heavens—and
no shrub of the field had yet appeared on the earth and no plant
of the field had yet sprung up, for the LORD God had not sent
rain on the earth and there was no man to work the ground, but
streams came up from the earth and watered the whole surface of
the ground—the LORD God formed the man from the dust of
the ground and breathed into his nostrils the breath of life, and
the man became a living being.

Now the LORD God had planted a garden in the east, in
Eden; and there he put the man he had formed. And the LORD
God made all kinds of trees grow out of the ground—trees that
were pleasing to the eye and good for food. In the middle of the
garden were the tree of life and the tree of the knowledge of good
and evil. (Genesis 2:4-9)

So Adam and Eve were in the Garden of Eden. Everything was
cool. But for some reason He put them in close proximity to the tree
of the knowledge of good and evil. He warned them not to eat the
fruit from this tree.

Adam and Eve had no idea what evil was. Why? Because they
were the furthest thing from it. They had no selfishness in their soul,
no ulterior motives in their hearts. They had nothing but love for
God, His creatures, His creation, and each other. While God created
both Adam and Eve with the freedom to choose to obey or disobey,
up to this point they had chosen what was right every time.

But then something happened in Genesis 3 that would rock the
course of history forever. Check it out:

Now the serpent was more crafty than any of the wild animals the
LORD God had made. He said to the woman, "Did God really
say, 'You must not eat from any tree in the garden'?"

The woman said to the serpent, "We may eat fruit from the trees in the garden, but God did say, 'You must not eat fruit from the tree that is in the middle of the garden, and you must not touch it, or you will die.' "

"You will not surely die," the serpent said to the woman. "For God knows that when you eat of it your eyes will be opened, and you will be like God, knowing good and evil."

When the woman saw that the fruit of the tree was good for food and pleasing to the eye, and also desirable for gaining wisdom, she took some and ate it. She also gave some to her husband, who was with her, and he ate it. (Genesis 3:1-6)

The serpent (who is really Satan in disguise . . . more on him in the next chapter) lied to Eve, and she began to question whether God was somehow holding back on her and Adam by keeping them from having their eyes opened and being like Him.

> **BLAST FROM THE PAST**
>
> It is impossible for one to live without tears, who considers things exactly as they are.[1]
>
> —GREGORY OF NYSSA, 4TH CENTURY BISHOP

Adam and Eve sinned, and as soon as they did, evil and its consequences invaded the human experience. This passage below is especially long but worth the read. It holds the key to how evil made its way onto planet Earth.

Then the eyes of both of them were opened, and they realized they were naked; so they sewed fig leaves together and made coverings for themselves.

Then the man and his wife heard the sound of the LORD God as he was walking in the garden in the cool of the day, and they hid from the LORD God among the trees of the garden. But the LORD God called to the man, "Where are you?"

He answered, "I heard you in the garden, and I was afraid

because I was naked; so I hid."

And he said, "Who told you that you were naked? Have you eaten from the tree that I commanded you not to eat from?"

The man said, "The woman you put here with me—she gave me some fruit from the tree, and I ate it."

Then the LORD God said to the woman, "What is this you have done?" The woman said, "The serpent deceived me, and I ate."

So the LORD God said to the serpent, "Because you have done this,

"Cursed are you above all the livestock
and all the wild animals!
You will crawl on your belly
and you will eat dust
all the days of your life.
And I will put enmity
between you and the woman,
and between your offspring and hers;
he will crush your head,
and you will strike his heel."

To the woman he said,

"I will greatly increase your pains in childbear-
ing; with pain you will give birth to children.

Your desire will be for your husband, and he
will rule over you."

To Adam he said, "Because you listened to your wife and ate from the tree about which I commanded you, 'You must not eat of it,'

"Cursed is the ground because of you;
through painful toil you will eat of it
all the days of your life.
It will produce thorns and thistles for you,

and you will eat the plants of the field.

By the sweat of your brow

you will eat your food

until you return to the ground,

since from it you were taken;

for dust you are

and to dust you will return."

Adam named his wife Eve, because she would become the mother of all the living.

The LORD God made garments of skin for Adam and his wife and clothed them. And the LORD God said, "The man has now become like one of us, knowing good and evil. He must not be allowed to reach out his hand and take also from the tree of life and eat, and live forever." So the LORD God banished him from the Garden of Eden to work the ground from which he had been taken. After he drove the man out, he placed on the east side of the Garden of Eden cherubim and a flaming sword flashing back and forth to guard the way to the tree of life. (Genesis 3:7-24)

Poisoned.

Adam and Eve chose to disobey the commandment of God, and as soon as they ate the fruit, they were poisoned. They were poisoned by sin. With one bite of fruit the toxin invaded every pore of their souls. They immediately tried to reverse the effects of the poison by covering their shame with fig-leaf clothing and by hiding in the garden.

INSANE BRAIN STRAIN

Why do bad things happen to both innocent, nice people and guilty, evil people? Why doesn't God use His power to allow the worst stuff to happen to the evilest people and give a pass to the people who are trying to live a good life?

But God found them and judged them. The judgment? Pain and suffering while on this side of eternity and expulsion from His intimate presence in the garden.

Through Adam's sin, physical pain entered the world. Now work and childbirth would be difficult. Not only that, but the world itself was infected with the poison of the consequences of Adam's sin. Weeds entered the world. But most notably, physical death entered the world, and the first thing to die was the innocent animal that God had to sacrifice to clothe Adam and Eve before He ushered them out of the garden.

The poison of Adam's sin brought evil, pain, and death onto this planet. Every child ever born (except Jesus) has been infected by the poison of Adam's sin. Romans 5:12 makes this clear: "Sin entered the world through one man, and death through sin."

Go Figure!

Open your Bible and read the first two chapters of Job.

1. What evil things happened to Job?

_____

_____

_____

2. Who was directly behind all the bad things that happened to Job?

_____

_____

_____

_____

3. Is this a case of bad things happening to good people? Why or why not?

_____

_____

_____

4. Why do you think God allowed Satan to attack Job?

_____

_____

_____

5. What gave Job the strength to keep his faith in God?

_____

_____

_____

6. How would you react if a series of bad events happened to you?

_____

_____

_____

The problem with the question raised in this chapter's Insane Brain Strain is that because of Adam and Eve and the sin with which they poisoned us all, there are no innocent people. As we learned from the last chapter, we all fall short of God's standard of perfection. We are all guilty in the courtroom of God.

As a result of Adam and Eve's sin, death, pain, and evil entered the world. Hitler, hurricanes, terrorists, tornados, tsunamis, and genocide are all a result of their disobedience to God.

So now that we see how evil entered the world, it's time to answer the question of why God would allow that to happen in the first place.

One reason is "free will." Adam and Eve were created with a will that was free to obey or disobey God. God could have made Adam and Eve obedient drones that simply did what they were told without question. He could have made them a kind of robot that mindlessly says yes to its programmer every time. He could have made us the same way. But He wanted Adam and Eve to obey Him out of choice, out of love. Instead they chose to sin.

God allowed evil in the world to give humanity the choice of whether or not to obey Him, and when that evil entered our ranks, God used it to demonstrate His power and grace.

We see His power demonstrated throughout human history. In spite of humanity's continual tendency toward sin and destruction, He continually redeems all of mankind's messes. Here are just a few instances of God demonstrating His power:

God delivered Noah and his family from a worldwide flood, which was brought on by humanity's rebellion against God.

God chose Abraham to father a nation. This nation became a shining light to the other nations and demonstrated that hope comes through God alone.

God rescued this nation, now called Israel, from the wickedness of Egypt and brought the Israelites into their own Promised Land.

Later on God rescued Israel from the wickedness of the Medes and Persians and brought them back into the Promised Land.

God sent His own Son to die for the sins of humanity and rescued us once and for all from the grip of sin.

God allowed evil to invade planet earth, and when it did, He showed us His power and grace. This grace is ultimately seen in the sacrifice of Jesus on the cross for our sins. Check this out:

For just as through the disobedience of the one man the many
were made sinners, so also through the obedience of the one man
the many will be made righteous.

The law was added so that the trespass might increase. But
where sin increased, grace increased all the more, so that, just as
sin reigned in death, so also grace might reign through righteousness to bring eternal life through Jesus Christ our Lord. (Romans
5:19-21)

God did not cause evil to be in this world, but He allowed it to
happen, then He redeemed His children with the blood of His own
Son. He allowed evil knowing that Jesus would triumph over it.

We have all been poisoned by sin. If you are a believer in Christ
then you have received the antidote. But the full effects of this antidote won't be fully felt until we are on the other side of eternity. Until
then, no matter what evil befalls us, we need to remember that the
antidote is found in Jesus Christ and, ultimately, He will crush all the
evil under His feet.

Be patient.

So What?

The complete answer to "why would God allow evil" might never be
answered in this life, but knowing that most of the evil in the world
is a result of sin and/or bad choices should help give you a better
understanding of this difficult issue. Also, knowing that God is in
complete control and will ultimately work out things for the best
should give you hope when it seems like everything is out of control.

YOU'RE NEXT!

Imagine you just received a letter/e-mail from a friend that said something like this:

Hey there—

Okay, so I have a serious question for you. It seems like every time I turn on the television or go on the Internet, there's story after story and image after image of tragedy, disease, war, famine, disasters, and death. I can't seem to make any sense out of this senseless world, but I know that you're a Christian and you believe in God—so I thought maybe you might have some answers to my questions . . . so here goes:

If there is a God, why is there so much evil in the world?

If God is truly God, why doesn't He do something about all the tragedy and death?

What do Christians think when tragedy happens?

Yeah, I know, simple questions—right? But I would really appreciate if you took some time and gave me your take on all this . . . thanks so much!

Write an imaginary letter/e-mail back to your friend using what you learned in this chapter.

_____

_____

_____

_____

_____

_____

_____

_____

_____

_____

_____

_____

_____

_____

_____

_____

_____

_____

_____

_____

For more info on **The Big Q: Why does God allow evil in this world?** visit www.dare2share.org/soulfuel/archives and check out *Soul Fuel* question #11.

CHAPTER 5

Demon Dogs Are After Me

Brown Elementary was about a 10-block walk (or run, if some kids were chasing me) from my house. When I was seven years old, every day was a challenge. Some kids in my neighborhood didn't like me—but that wasn't my biggest worry. I also had to walk to school through major snowstorms, which made my walk long and cold. But that didn't bother me at all.

What did bother me were the two German shepherds that often ran loose along my route to school. The people who owned them didn't seem concerned that their dogs escaped regularly. I'm sure they didn't think that these dogs would ever hurt anybody. But I wasn't sure. These dogs looked vicious, as if they wanted to eat a second-grader for breakfast. I was always careful to walk on the other side of the street. And I tried to be as quiet as I could. The last thing I wanted was for them to hear me, then come running across the street and attack me.

One cold Colorado day I was making my daily trek to Brown Elementary when out of the corner of my eye something caught my attention. The two German shepherds had escaped again, but this time they were headed at full speed straight for me. My heart was pounding like a drum as I backed up to a chain-link fence and prayed.

These dogs were going to attack. I knew it. They weren't barking, they were charging. Without thinking, I crossed my arms in front of my face and grabbed the chain-link fence with my tiny fingers. I was standing with my arms blocking my face and holding on with all my might to the cold metal of the fence.

One dog was going toward my face, and the other dog was trying to attack my stomach or arms or something. I couldn't really tell. I only knew they were biting me hard and it hurt. I soon realized that if I let go of that fence and the bigger dog got hold of my face, I would be in even more trouble. If they had gotten hold of my throat, they could have killed me.

Oh yeah, I left out one important detail. I was wearing a thick leather jacket that was zipped up to the top (thanks, Ma!), so the dogs, while they left indentations from their teeth all over my arms, couldn't penetrate my skin.

Finally a wiry, little old lady nicknamed "Ma" Zeemer came out with a baseball bat (my second experience with a bat!) and chased those dirty dogs away. She told the police the attack went on for minutes. It took her that long to shuffle down the street to come to my aid. The police officers made sure I was all right and then sent me on my way.

It's weird. I never saw those dogs again. Years later Grandma told me why. That night when my grandpa heard what had happened, he went to their owner's door and knocked. Grandma told me that the conversation went something like this:

"Did you know that my grandson was attacked by your two dogs this morning?"

"Yeah, so what?"

"Well, I just want to show you my .357 Magnum pistol here. It's got three bullets in it, two for your dogs and one for you—if I ever see those dogs again."

Does it seem weird to you that here I was, a seven-year-old kid, who had already had so many brushes with death? One threat happened while I was still in my mother's womb, the next in an emergency room with appendicitis. The close calls came from jumping through a window and being attacked for several minutes by two German shepherd dogs.

It seemed as if someone was trying to kill me. And I have had several brushes with death since. For instance, I've been in nine car crashes since I got my driver's license. What if somebody really is trying to kill me? Maybe not just dogs . . . but demons. Maybe they want you dead, too?

Wild as this may sound, they actually do.

How do I know? Because Jesus told us their ringleader wants us dead: "The thief comes only to steal and kill and destroy; I have come that they may have life, and have it to the full" (John 10:10).

Satan and his gang of spiritual thugs want to steal your joy, kill your body, and destroy your faith. They hate you. They hate everything about you. They want to see you self-medicate, self-mutilate, and self-destruct.

> **BLAST FROM THE PAST**
>
> Many do not recognize the fact as they ought, that Satan has got men fast asleep in sin and that it is his great device to keep them so.[1]
>
> —CATHERINE BOOTH, 19TH CENTURY MOTHER OF THE SALVATION ARMY

They cheer when you assume the identity of someone else on MySpace so that you can talk about things you would never talk about with your youth group friends. They applaud your failed attempts at reading the Bible on a consistent basis. When you trip up spiritually, they laugh and slap high-fives all around.

※ ※ ※

The Big Q: Who are Satan and his demons?

Believe it or not, Satan and his demons didn't start out evil—but they became evil. Before history was written, Satan was the right-hand angel of God. He was God's number-one homeboy. Listen to how God describes Satan before he turned bad:

> "You were the model of perfection,
> full of wisdom and perfect in beauty.
> You were in Eden,
> the garden of God;
> every precious stone adorned you:
> ruby, topaz and emerald,
> chrysolite, onyx and jasper,
> sapphire, turquoise and beryl.
> Your settings and mountings were made of gold;
> on the day you were created they were prepared.
> You were anointed as a guardian cherub,
> for so I ordained you.
> You were on the holy mount of God;
> you walked among the fiery stones.
> You were blameless in your ways
> from the day you were created
> till wickedness was found in you."
> (Ezekiel 28:12-15)

Before Satan became Satan he was "the model of perfection." He set the standard of what it meant to be an angel. He was "full of wisdom and perfect in beauty." He was wicked smart and drop-dead gorgeous. He was decked out in the best jewels and was considered a guardian of God's throne. He had access to the very presence of God.

But one day he found a mirror . . . or something. He began to look at himself instead of at God. He noticed how smart he was, how beautiful he was, how powerful he was, and how much face-time he had with God. Pride erupted in his heart, and he began to think he could rule heaven in the place of Jesus.

Go Figure!

Check out Isaiah 14:12-15 to find out how Satan's pride brought him down. Read the passage in your Bible, then answer these questions:

1. What are the five "I wills" that Satan said in his heart?

   _____

   _____

   _____

2. From this passage do you think that Satan thought he could really overthrow God and take over heaven?

   _____

   _____

   _____

3. Why are these "I wills" the result of a deceived mind?

   _____

   _____

   _____

4. If you could describe Satan's sin in this passage with one word, what word would it be?

_____

_____

_____

5. In what ways do you struggle with the same sin when it comes to, not who rules heaven, but who rules you?

_____

_____

_____

Somewhere during this whole process Satan began to recruit other angels to follow him. He was aligning his forces to take over heaven. Surely he could take over the throne of God.

But then God flexed.

Satan and his angels were evicted from heaven. We know them now as the devil and his demons. Basically they are fallen angels with a vendetta against God and against us.

Why us?

Because we as Christians receive for free what they failed to gain by force: the kingdom of God.

 INSANE BRAIN STRAIN

If the most powerful being ever created couldn't replace God as the Ruler of the universe, where do we get the idea that we can replace Him as the Ruler of our lives?

So they attack relentlessly, and they will continue to do so until that day Jesus shows them His power (like my grandpa showed his .357 Magnum) and banishes them to hell forever. Check out Revelation 20:10: "And the devil, who deceived [the nations], was thrown into the lake of burning sulfur, where the beast and the false prophet had been thrown. They will be tormented day and night for ever and ever."

So What?

If you knew there was a pack of wild dogs just around the corner, would you avoid them at all costs? Of course! And if you couldn't avoid the dogs, would you prepare yourself for their attacks? Duh! The fact is, you truly have demon dogs after you, waiting for your guard to come down so they can attack and try to shred you to pieces. You can protect yourself by avoiding tempting situations and preparing for the attacks by staying close to Christ by reading the Bible and re-maining in a constant state of prayer.

Until the day Jesus throws the devil into the lake of fire, put on your armor and get ready to fight these demon dogs with the baseball bat that God has provided you. More on that later. . . .

YOU'RE NEXT!

In Isaiah 14:12-14 the Bible gives us insight into what was behind Satan's fall from heaven:

> How you have fallen from heaven,
>> O morning star, son of the dawn!
>> You have been cast down to the earth,
>> you who once laid low the nations!

You said in your heart,
> "I will ascend to heaven;
> I will raise my throne
> above the stars of God;
> I will sit enthroned on the mount of assembly,
> on the utmost heights of the sacred mountain.
> I will ascend above the tops of the clouds;
> I will make myself like the Most High."

If you look carefully, you'll notice that there are five statements that begin with the phrase "I will." These exclaim a prideful rebellion against God. Satan let his pride grow and grow until he actually thought he was greater than God. The same thing can happen to us, which is why we need to always be on our guard against pride. One great remedy for a proud heart is a humble action plan, so take a few minutes and make a new list of "I wills" that reflect your desire to worship and serve God instead of yourself each and every day. For example:

- I will start each day praising God.
- I will study His Word so I know His desires for my life.
- I will resist the one who tempts me to rebel against God.

_____

_____

_____

_____

_____

_____

_____

_____

_____

_____

✳ ✳ ✳

For more info on **The Big Q: Who are Satan and his demons?** visit www.dare2share.org/soulfuel/archives and check out *Soul Fuel* question #20.

CHAPTER 6

Jack and Jesus

All my uncles were tough. But the essence of buff, rough, and tough was Uncle Jack. I've never met another guy in my life like him. I've met bigger guys with more tattoos . . . but I've never encountered someone who was so much "the whole package" as Uncle Jack.

He had big muscles. Jack was a bodybuilder, a power lifter, and an arm wrestler. Though only 185 pounds he was extremely strong in the gym and to this day can hold his own—and he is over 70 years old!

He had a big attitude. There was nobody, I mean *nobody*, whom Jack would back down from in a fistfight. Jack, like my mom, was mad at something, at everything. There was a deep inner rage that fueled and focused him in every fight.

As a result of his inner Hulk, he fought anybody and everybody . . . even police officers. One day two police officers came to arrest him at his house, and he beat them both senseless. When other patrolmen arrived on the scene they "applied" the billy club to finally restrain him. He was coughing up blood for days. Instead of jail he spent three months in a mental institution.

From the time Jack was a teenager he lived on the wrong side of the law and by the right hook of his fist. Jack was a force of nature.

But some forces are bigger than even Jack.

There was that day in the early 1970s when a preacher nick-named "Yankee" came to Jack's house on a dare to tell him about Jesus. When Jack answered the door he had no shirt, and a beer can was in each hand (one to drink beer out of and the other to spit tobacco chew into). At Jack's side was the biggest German shepherd that you could imagine.

After some small talk the preacher asked him if he could take five minutes, come into the house, and tell him about Jesus and how Jack could know for sure that he was going to heaven someday.

Jack obliged.

Over the next five minutes Jack began to understand the gospel for the first time. He began to understand the real Jesus for the first time.

When the preacher asked him, "Will you trust in Jesus right now as your only hope of going to heaven?" Jack simply exclaimed, "Hell, yeah!" That was his "sinner's prayer." He went from fighting thug to witnessing thug overnight. And when I say witnessing thug, I'm not kidding.

He started sharing the gospel (sometimes laced with curse words because he didn't know any better) with anybody and everybody. Now instead of throwing fists at somebody, he was throwing verses at everybody. He told all of his bodybuilder, tough guy, motorcycle, thug friends. And then he started telling complete strangers.

One day he even went into a Mormon church on a Sunday morning, asked where the newcomer's Sunday school class was, and made an appearance there. The teacher assumed he was a recent con-vert to Mormonism. At least he thought that until Jack got up and started sharing the gospel. After Jack spoke, most all of the 20 or so new Mormons in the class became new Christians that day.

What was the reason for this radical transformation? Simple. Jack met somebody tougher than he was. He met the Lord Jesus Christ.

You see, the Jesus that Jack knew of before he became a Christian was a religious, safe, stained-glass Jesus. But the Jesus that Yankee introduced to Jack was anything but safe and nothing even close to religious.

This Jesus was intense. Although He raged against the religious, He partied with the sinners. While He never condoned their sin or sinned, He showed the partiers of His time (tax collectors and prostitutes) how to really have a good time, by fully following after Him.

This Jesus was tough. Two separate times, once at the beginning of His earthly ministry and once at the end, Jesus' outrage erupted as He flipped over countless tables of the lying, cheating moneychangers selling in the temple. We're talking maybe hundreds or perhaps even thousands. He was a man nobody tried to stop. He was so full of rage over their sin they just ran from this wildman from God.

This Jesus was loving. He talked to the destitute. He preached compassion. He fed the poor. He hugged the children. He touched the sick, the blind, the crippled, and even the lepers. He touched them and healed them because He was full of compassion.

The intense, tough, and loving Jesus who transformed Uncle Jack was more than just a mere man. Much more.

The Big Q: Who is Jesus?

Jesus is 100 percent God and 100 percent man. He is not 50 percent of each but 100 percent of both. Before He was born of a virgin He was ruling in heaven. He was worshiped and adored by millions upon millions of angels all the time. Why? Because He was the Creator and Ruler of the universe!

But two thousand years ago He got up off His throne, wrapped Himself in a coat of skin, and became Jesus, the God-man. He is 100 percent God and 100 percent man. Why is that important? Because as a man He could die for other men, and as God that payment for sin was infinite!

Here's how Philippians 2:5-11 puts it:

Your attitude should be the same as that of Christ Jesus:
Who, being in very nature God,
did not consider equality with God something to be grasped,
but made himself nothing,
taking the very nature of a servant,
being made in human likeness.
And being found in appearance as a man,
he humbled himself
and became obedient to death—
even death on a cross!
Therefore God exalted him to the highest place
and gave him the name that is above every name,
that at the name of Jesus every knee should bow,
in heaven and on earth and under the earth,
and every tongue confess that Jesus Christ is Lord,
to the glory of God the Father.

Jesus gave up the adoration of angels and exchanged it for the mockery of mankind. He gave up being worshiped and adored by all of heaven as God to be questioned and eventually killed by a skeptical humanity.

How do we know that Jesus was fully God? Because He claimed to be God and then proved it by His resurrection! But He was also fully man.

Did you know that one of the first false teachings that plagued the early church asserted that Jesus only *seemed* to be human? This

"cult" (a group of people who distort the teaching of God's Word)
preached a message that Jesus was fully God, but didn't have a real
body of flesh, bone, muscle, sinew, and blood like you and me. The
apostle John took on these false teachers in 1 John 4:1-3:

> Dear friends, do not believe every spirit, but test the spirits to see
> whether they are from God, because many false prophets have
> gone out into the world. This is how you can recognize the Spirit
> of God: Every spirit that acknowledges that Jesus Christ has
> come in the flesh is from God, but every spirit that does not
> acknowledge Jesus is not from God.

This passage reminds us all that Jesus' being fully human is every
bit as important as Him being divine. Not only does John remind us
of Jesus' humanity, but so does Luke:

> While they were still talking about this, Jesus himself stood
> among them and said to them, "Peace be with you." They were
> startled and frightened, thinking they saw a ghost. He said to
> them, "Why are you troubled, and why do doubts rise in your
> minds? Look at my hands and my feet. It is I myself! Touch me
> and see; a ghost does not have flesh and bones, as you see I have."
> When he had said this, he showed them his hands and feet.
> And while they still did not believe it because of joy and amaze-
> ment, he asked them, "Do you have anything here to eat?" They
> gave him a piece of broiled fish, and he took it and ate it in their
> presence. (24:36-43)

After Jesus' resurrection, the disciples freaked when they saw
Him. They thought He was a ghost (wouldn't you if your best friend
showed up at your doorstep after his funeral?). To prove that He had

a real body, He invited the disciples to touch Him. Finally He ate some food in their presence to prove that His body was real.

Go Figure!

Open your Bible to John 8:48-59 and read it carefully. As you do, remember that Jesus lived two thousand years after Abraham, then answer these questions:

1. How do we know these particular Jews were upset with Jesus?

_____

_____

_____

2. What did Jesus say about how Abraham viewed Him, and how did the Jews respond?

_____

_____

_____

3. What was Jesus claiming with His statement "I AM"? (Go back and read Exodus 3:14 if you don't remember what it says.)

_____

_____

_____

4. How do we know that the Jews understood Jesus was making a radical statement when He said "I AM"?

_____

_____

_____

5. If Jesus was lying about being God, would you be able to trust His other claims? Why or why not?

_____

_____

    You may have heard that Jesus never claimed to be God, but nothing could be further from the truth. Not only did He claim to be God; He claimed God's personal name "I AM" as His own in John 8:58! (Go back and review chapter 1 if you don't remember this.) And this is not the only verse where Jesus claims to be God. Check out these verses:

Philip said, "Lord, show us the Father and that will be enough for us."

    Jesus answered: "Don't you know me, Philip, even after I have been among you such a long time? Anyone who has seen me has seen the Father. How can you say, "Show us the Father"? (John 14:8-9)

[Jesus said,] "I give them eternal life, and they shall never perish; no one can snatch them out of my hand. My Father, who has given them to me, is greater than all; no one can snatch them out of my Father's hand. I and the Father are one."

    Again the Jews picked up stones to stone him, but Jesus said to them, "I have shown you many great miracles from the Father. For which of these do you stone me?"

    "We are not stoning you for any of these," replied the Jews, "but for blasphemy, because you, a mere man, claim to be God." (John 10:28-33)

Not only did Jesus claim to be God, but ultimately He proved it through His resurrection from the dead. After Jesus rose from the dead, here is how one of His disciples responded when he saw Him for the first time:

> Jesus came and stood among them and said, "Peace be with you!" Then he said to Thomas, "Put your finger here; see my hands. Reach out your hand and put it into my side. Stop doubting and believe."
>
> Thomas said to him, "My Lord and my God!"
>
> Then Jesus told him, "Because you have seen me, you have believed; blessed are those who have not seen and yet have believed." (John 20:26-29)

Notice that Jesus never rebukes Thomas for calling Him Lord and God. Instead, He rebukes him for not believing this earlier.

Jesus was fully God and fully man, yet without sin. How could this be? Because God supernaturally placed the unborn life of Jesus in Mary's womb. As a result, Adam's poison of sin was never passed to Jesus! So Jesus, although human, was not sinful. The book of Hebrews makes this clear. Speaking of Jesus the author writes, "For we do not have a high priest who is unable to sympathize with our weaknesses, but we have one who has been tempted in every way, just as we are—yet was without sin" (Hebrews 4:15).

INSANE BRAIN STRAIN

Jesus had a human nature and a divine nature but not a sinful nature. Check out Luke 22:39-44 to see the inner struggle He had in the Garden of Gethsemane between His human and divine wills. Yet He submitted both in the end to the Father's will. He was tempted, yet was without sin. By the way, this means Jesus can relate to our struggle. He's been tempted by sin, too! He's just never given in to it!

So What?

Because Jesus is 100 percent human, He can totally relate to every thought, feeling, joy, pain, trial, and even temptation that you are going through. Jesus experienced life at its full intensity on every level, so there's nothing in your life He can't connect with and understand. Because Jesus is 100 percent God, He can give you the strength to control your thoughts and feelings, experience joy to the fullest, walk you through your pains and trials, and lead you away from temptation. Don't hesitate to take every aspect of your life to Christ, because it's not as if anything is going to catch Him by surprise!

And guess what? When you pray to God the Father in the name of Jesus, you are coming to God with the authority of the most precious thing in the universe to God, His only Son. You are pulling on God's heartstrings when you pray in the name of Jesus. In our prayers the mere presence of Jesus at the right hand of God becomes our most powerful asset. Because the Father loves the Son, and because the Son relates to us in our weakness, God will give us the grace and strength we need to live our life to the fullest!

The intense, tough, and loving Jesus who transformed Uncle Jack was bigger and more powerful than any force my uncle had ever met

> **BLAST FROM THE PAST**
>
> A man who was merely a man and said the sort of things Jesus said would not be a great moral teacher. He would either be a lunatic—on a level with the man who says he is a poached egg—or else he would be the Devil of Hell. You must make your choice. Either this man was, and is, the Son of God: or else a madman or something worse. You can shut Him up for a fool, you can spit at Him and kill Him as a demon; or you can fall at His feet and call Him Lord and God. But let us not come with any patronizing nonsense about His being a great human teacher. He has not left that open to us. He did not intend to.[1]
>
> —C. S. Lewis, 20th century writer

before. Are you allowing God to be big and powerful in your life? All I know is this: If Jesus could reach Jack, He can reach anybody.

YOU'RE NEXT!

Jesus as a human knows exactly how temptation feels. Jesus as God knows exactly how to conquer temptation. Take a few minutes and complete the sentences below. (Use a separate piece of paper if you want to keep your list private.)

Because Jesus is human, He can relate to my temptations in the following areas:

_____

_____

_____

Because Jesus is God, He can give me the power to conquer these temptations, so here is my prayer to God in Jesus' name:

Dear God,

_____

_____

_____

_____

_____

_____

_____

In Jesus' name I pray. Amen.

✳ ✳ ✳

For more info on **The Big Q: Who is Jesus?** visit www.dare2 share.org/soulfuel/archives and check out *Soul Fuel* question #3.

CHAPTER 7

Hell Made Me Pee My Pants

Hell made me pee my pants—literally.

I'll never forget it. I was seven years old, walking back home from good old Brown Elementary. No kids were chasing me. No dogs were chasing me. But some pretty morbid thoughts about hell were chasing me.

I had heard a teaching on hell from the pastor or Sunday school teacher at the Baptist church where I attended with my grandparents. The message got garbled in my heart and head, and what I heard was this: "If you confess all your sins to God, you can be delivered from the eternal flames of hell."

I thought that I had to literally confess, not only that I was a sinner, but all my specific sins. I thought if I missed confessing even one, I'd go to hell. The more I thought about hell, the more scared I got. The more scared I got, the more sins I confessed. The more sins I confessed, the more I cussed.

You see, I was a neurotic little kid. And my neurosis spilled over into my prayers. It went something like:

Dear God, I know that I'm a sinner. I confess all my sins. I confess last week when I yelled at my brother. I confess that I didn't make my bed the other day. I confess that I was daydreaming at school today. I think that is it! So, I've confessed all my sins . . . I think.

And then out of nowhere a curse word would appear in my mind, and I would say it in my head, "x@!*&!"

So I'd confess the curse word, and then another worse curse word would appear in my mind. So I'd confess it. I had heard a lot of those words from my family members, so this whole process went on and on in an endless cycle of self-induced despair.

I thought if I died between the cussing and the confession of the cussing that I'd go straight to hell. It was somewhere in the midst of this confused confession and cursing that I finally lost it—control of my bladder, that is. I had been so consumed with my confession and the impending doom of hell that peeing my pants didn't seem so bad.

The Big Q: Are there a real heaven and hell, and what are they like?

Thus began my search for the eternal realities of understanding heaven and hell. Let's start with hell. I readily admit I have a serious problem with the doctrine of hell. It's hard to imagine a loving God who would create an eternal place of suffering for sinners. Don't get me wrong; I think that sinners should suffer some. But an eternity of agony in "fire and brimstone" for all those who happen not to be Christians? Come on!

It's a lot easier to imagine hell as a place where people are not physically tortured but psychologically tormented until they regret and repent. Maybe at this point they are even given a second chance to respond to Christ. This kind of hell seems to have the best of both worlds: Sinners are punished and then mercy is demonstrated. Perhaps the exception to this rule is the worst of the worst sinners. Those who commit mass murder in the name of some warped ideology like Hitler and Stalin could burn forever as far as I'm concerned.

Or maybe hell could be mere annihilation—eternal extinction of the soul, if you will. When people are plunged into that infernal inferno, it is a final purging of existence, and they cease to be. As horrible as that may sound, it is infinitely more fathomable than an *eternal* hell.

I have a problem with accepting a doctrine that condemns the sinner to a forever future without hope, without escape, without a second chance. To be honest, my heart begins to hurt and my brain starts to ache when I think about it. Questions flood my mind and challenge my convictions, questions like how could a loving God send people to an eternity in fire and brimstone? And if God is so merciful why would He cause people to suffer for so long in such pain?

But no matter how many times I try to explain hell away or redefine and make it palatable to my puny brain, there it is in black and white again and again throughout the pages of the Bible. No matter how I try to imagine it away or tone it down, one thing is clear: The Bible describes hell as for real and forever.[1]

Go Figure!

Read Luke 16:19-31 and answer these questions:

1. How does the rich man describe his suffering?

   _____

   _____

   _____

2. Does his suffering seem like real suffering in real flames?

   _____

   _____

   _____

3. What shows that the rich man's situation is inescapable?

   _____

   _____

   _____

4. Why is he concerned for his brothers?

   _____

   _____

   _____

5. How should the rich man's concern impact the way we see our unreached friends?

   _____

   _____

   _____

Jesus throws kerosene on the flames when He speaks so matter-of-factly about a literal hell. Did you know that the Son of God spoke more about hell than heaven? Of the 12 times that hell is described in the New Testament, 11 are mentioned by Jesus. And He never described hell as figurative, temporary, or anything less than horrific. Five different times He calls it a place of "weeping and gnashing of teeth." I'm not even sure what gnashing of teeth is, but it doesn't sound pleasant. Maybe peeing my pants at the thought of hell wasn't as childish as I thought . . .

Speaking of unpleasant thoughts, check out these two passages about hell:

> He will punish those who do not know God and do not obey
> the gospel of our Lord Jesus. They will be punished with ever-
> lasting destruction and shut out from the presence of the Lord
> and from the majesty of his power. (2 Thessalonians 1:8-9)

> He, too, will drink of the wine of God's fury, which has been
> poured full strength into the cup of his wrath. He will be tor-
> mented with burning sulfur in the presence of the holy angels
> and of the Lamb. And the smoke of their torment rises for ever
> and ever. There is no rest day or night. (Revelation 14:10-11)

The list of verses goes on and on and on. From the Old Testament to the New Testament, hell is described with real and raw adjectives as your worst fears come true and are multiplied by infinity for eternity.

Here is where the troubling question rears its ugly head once again. How could a loving God send people whom He created to suffer in an eternal hell?

And maybe that question is the problem. Oftentimes the twenty-first-century version of the Christian God is "just loving" instead of "just *and* loving." The "just" part of God (that demands absolute justice, holiness, perfection) has been minimized and the "loving" part of God (that shows mercy, grace, and forgiveness) has been maximized.

While many Christians believe in an eternal hell, they usually don't bring it up much. It is unpleasant and leads to too many questions about the character of God. Hell is that crazy doctrine that we keep locked in the basement of our belief systems. We all know that it is there, chained to the underbelly of the theology of the holiness of God. We hope that it stays in the shadows and never comes up in conversation. Why? Because if people found out what we really believed they would think we were radicals, extremists, and kooks.

Or maybe they wouldn't.

Perhaps it would confirm their deepest fears. Maybe it would bring to light thoughts that they try to keep locked in the inner recesses of their souls. Thoughts like, *What if there is an afterlife? What if there is a heaven and hell? Which one will I be going to when I die?*

 ## INSANE BRAIN STRAIN

Hell is forever, without escape.

Our God is a holy God who lit the fires of hell with His hatred for sin. Our God is a loving God who sent His own Son to die on a cross so that we wouldn't have to go there. And therein lies the paradox of the gospel message and of the Christian God: He is not "just loving" but "just *and* loving."

So it turns out that my problem with hell is my problem. The Bible has no problem with it, nor does Jesus. So I must accept the doctrine even though it grates against my own logic. And what are the implications?

No-holds-barred evangelism. Like it or not.

So what about heaven?

Jesus said in John 14:1-3, "Do not let your hearts be troubled. Trust in God; trust also in me. In my Father's house are many rooms; if it were not so, I would have told you. I am going there to prepare a place for you. And if I go and prepare a place for you, I will come back and take you to be with me that you also may be where I am."

Think about what Jesus is saying in these verses. First of all He is reminding us not to be troubled because in a very short time we are going to be in heaven! The whole idea of heaven is to give us hope! We have something to look forward to that is well beyond anything we could ever imagine. Think of the best time you could ever have on this planet earth and then multiply it by a billion. Only then could you get a glimpse of the kind of fun heaven is going to be.

BLAST FROM THE PAST

William Booth, founder of The Salvation Army, once said that he wished he could take his leaders and dangle them over the flames of hell and that "if they could see the flames and smell the smoke and feel the heat and hear the cries of the damned, they would go out to preach what they had seen and heard. They would then preach like dying men to dying people."[2]

Secondly, heaven is going to have a lot of room and a lot of rooms. And guess what? There's a space and place for you and me. Jesus Himself is designing a special place for you and me and every believer in Christ who walked on this planet.

In this chapter's "Blast from the Past," William Booth indicated that hell was a powerful motivation to reach people with the gospel. But I think the motivation of heaven is even stronger. If you could take 10 Christian leaders and let them see the horrors of hell for 24 hours, those leaders would shake the world for Jesus when they got back to earth. But I am convinced if you could take just one Christian and let him/her see the glory of God for 24 seconds, this person would single-handedly reach the world with the gospel.

Why do I say that? Because it kind of already happened! Check out the words of the apostle Paul in 2 Corinthians 12:2-4. (Hint: The "man in Christ" is Paul; he's referring to himself.)

> I know a man in Christ who fourteen years ago was caught up to the third heaven. Whether it was in the body or out of the body I do not know—God knows. And I know that this man—whether in the body or apart from the body I do not know, but God knows—was caught up to paradise. He heard inexpressible things, things that man is not permitted to tell.

If there was ever one man who single-handedly shook the world for God it was the apostle Paul. What motivated him? I'm convinced that his primary motivational "fuel" came from what he saw in heaven. Whatever it was, it blew him away and gave him a glimpse of what is to come for every believer in Jesus.

So What?

Both heaven and hell should motivate us to believe in Jesus and share His message with everyone. These twin realities are the two cylinders that drive the engine of our motivation to evangelize everyone. We should be intense and intentional, sharing with urgency as though people's lives depend upon it—because they do.

Just don't pee your pants when you tell them.

YOU'RE NEXT!

Take a few minutes and initiate an electronic conversation with an unsaved friend about heaven and hell. To help you get started, read the following real IM conversation between two teens.

AlexMan89:   if u died now where would u go?

Razzz90:   haha. into a casket in the ground.

AlexMan89:   seriously

Razzz90:   yeah. when you're dead, you're still you... just not with your body. you're just yourself with your thoughts. once your body is dead, the way you acted is just meant to impact other peoples lives... it's not going to heaven or hell

AlexMan89:   ok so u dont believe in a heaven or hell

Razzz90:   no. not exactly.

AlexMan89:   wat if ur wrong? I mean if im wrong i just look stupid maybe. but if ur wrong, u spend eternity in hell

Razzz90:   but there is no eternity? if I don't believe in it, then how can it happen to me?

Razzz90:   wait. that's stupid. If I didn't believe in rape, it might still happen to me.

Razzz90:   i don't know. i guess when it happens i'll do something about it?

AlexMan89:   by then it'll be too late

AlexMan89:   when ur dead and ur at the gates of heaven u cant expect to put urself on the guest list, if ur not there u cant get into the party

Razzz90:   but God wouldn't put people on a guest list because he's supposed to be all perfect and forgiving of everyone?

AlexMan89:   ur right. he doesnt send anybody to hell, he loves us so much that he allows us to choose, he would like us to be there in heaven, but he's willing to let us decide to accept him or not even if that means u go to hell

Razzz90:   so I accept him but not Jesus... can I still go to heaven?

AlexMan89:   well that goes back to the holy trinity thing, jesus says i am the way the truth and the life no one comes to the father but through me

Razzz90:   sigh. it's so confusing.

AlexMan89:   religion makes it confusing, jesus dissed religion, he wants to have a relationship with u

AlexMan89:   so all u have to do is trust in jesus. Once u do that ur put on heaven's guest list

AlexMan89:   just pray and ask jesus to guide ur life, tell him that u believe that jesus died on the cross for all of our sins, and u want to trust in him and follow him and have ur sins forgiven because u want to be in heaven

Razzz90:   like no way? you so sounded like a little commercial there.

Razzz90:   just 19.99 and you can have a broom that picks up all the dirt!

AlexMan89:   thats right so really do u wanna pray it up or not

Razzz90:   haha. i guess. It won't cost anything.

AlexMan89:   nope. jesus paid the price when he died on the cross. Just pray c'mon

Razzz90:   i do pray. just not about believing in jesus.

AlexMan89:   y not? wat do u have to lose?

Razzz90:   because it's so impossible and corny. can't i just pray for other people and be
              thankful for things but not jesus?

AlexMan89:   u can, but sin cant be removed by good deeds, u still cant go to heaven by
              good deeds alone. U NEED jesus

Razzz90:   i guess i'm in need.

AlexMan89:   ya! so do u want to accept christ?

Razzz90:   Maybe.

AlexMan89:   there comes a time when u have to decide. u have to make a decision

AlexMan89:   theres no in between. heaven or hell

Razzz90:   what's so bad about hell anyways?

AlexMan89:   lets see: eternal pain . . . hmmm . . . sounds like a fun place

AlexMan89:   or heaven: eternal party

Razzz90:   Party party party. Jesus party.

AlexMan89:   all u have to do is trust in Jesus!

Razzz90:   i think i'm gonna go tell jesus that i want him in my life so you are happy and
              stop being a commercial man about it and so i can go have a party

AlexMan89:   its not about me

Razzz90:   it's about jesus and me. yes. . . . i get it.

✳ ✳ ✳

For more info on **The Big Q: Is there a real heaven and hell, and
what are they like?** visit www.dare2share.org/soulfuel/archives and
check out *Soul Fuel* question #16.

*My cousin Larry, an example of the family
bodybuilding gene pool I missed out on*

CHAPTER 8

Bob and God

He was mean. He was big. He could bench-press the house. My uncle Bob, at 6 foot 3 and 250 or so pounds, has always been a big, strapping, strong man.

For a while a lot of our family (aunts, uncles, cousins) lived in the same house on Irving Street in Denver. When Uncle Bob was there, I used to hide from him behind the couch a lot.

Why? Because he scared me to death! He would sometimes come home from his job with blood on his clothes from the latest person he had beat to a pulp. He was a cigar-chomping, wild-eyed street fighter who actually got paid to bust skulls. He was a bouncer at the Silver Dollar Bar and Grill in the heart of the city. Because of the especially rowdy type of customer this bar attracted, the owners needed an even tougher breed of bouncer. So they hired Bob.

One night Bob was at the bar when he heard there was a fight out in the parking lot. He ran outside only to find his best friend, D. J., bleeding from five stab wounds. Others were rushing to D. J.'s aid, so Bob went hunting for the culprit. He found him hiding on the outside of the building.

Bob ran up to the guy, smashed his head into the brick wall, and began pummeling him with his fists and kicking him with his feet. The intoxicated stabber never had a chance to pull his knife out or even really fight back.

Uncle Bob continued to beat him in a blind fury of rage until the cops finally arrived. By this time Bob was kicking a corpse. This thug's heart had stopped.

The police arrested Uncle Bob, put the cuffs on, and threw him into the back of the squad car. It was at this point, as he was looking out the window and seeing the paramedics trying to pump this guy's heart to start beating again, that Bob snapped out of his rage and back into reality.

For the first time he realized the full gravity of the situation. He had literally just beaten a guy to death and was probably going to go to jail for a long, long time, if not on first-degree murder charges, then for manslaughter.

In sheer desperation Bob began to cry out to God, "If You allow that man to be resuscitated, I will give my life completely to You and serve You with all of my heart!"

Just then the man's heart began to beat again. He survived and fully recovered.

Uncle Bob, who had trusted in Jesus as a little kid, got back on the narrow path that night. He stayed true to the promise he made to God in the back of the squad car. A year later he was attending Florida Bible College, and to this day he faithfully proclaims the message of Jesus to those around him. While Uncle Bob started down his life-changing path as a result of the near death and miraculous resuscitation of the drunk, violent criminal he beat up that night, he stayed on that path because his life was transformed by the death and resurrection of his Savior, Jesus Christ.

I'm struck by the sharp contrasts between these two powerful influences on Uncle Bob's life. First of all, the drunk guy may have deserved to die, but Jesus didn't. The inebriated man was full of anger and alcohol. Jesus was full of love and truth. This knife-wielding criminal was beaten badly and nearly died. This hope-wielding Savior was beaten badly and did die. One was resuscitated and the other resurrected.

The resurrected Christ transformed my uncle Bob for good. He rushed in, took over, and transformed. Whereas the drunken guy brought out the worst in my uncle Bob, the resurrected Jesus brought out the best—actually, He brought in the best.

It was the resurrected Jesus who transformed Uncle Bob from bar bouncer to Bible-thumper, from a cigar-chomping, rear-kicking madman into a Scripture-preaching, soul-shaking Jesus freak.

The Big Q: How do I know Jesus really rose from the dead?

If you were to ask me how I knew Jesus really rose from the dead I would simply say, "Because the Bible says so and because I've seen Him change Jack and Bob." That was enough for me as a child. I knew Jesus rose from the dead because I believed every word of the Bible, and I saw Him at work in changing lives all around me.

Over the years I have seen Him change countless lives. But I also have discovered that many people who don't believe in Jesus reject the whole changed-lives argument. So I began to dig a little deeper and was surprised at what I discovered.

BLAST FROM THE PAST

The resurrection is the keystone of the arch on which our faith is supported. If Christ has not risen, we must impeach all those witnesses for lying. If Christ has not risen, we have no proof that the crucifixion of Jesus differed from that of the two thieves who suffered with him. If Christ has not risen, it is impossible to believe his atoning death was accepted.[1]

—D. L. MOODY, 20TH CENTURY EVANGELIST

First of all I discovered that the Romans were experts at killing people. They killed them all the time. They knew how to execute criminals. As a matter of fact, one time they crucified six thousand people in one day![2]

When the soldier thrust the spear into Jesus' side and blood and water flowed out, they had all the proof they needed to know Jesus had died. Why? Because the "water" that flowed out was the liquid from the pericardium, the sac that surrounded the heart of Jesus. His heart had been pierced. His breathing had stopped. His life had been ended.

No doubt about it.

Then Jesus was taken down from the cross. His body was cleaned off, and then He was mummified (in the Jewish, not Egyptian, sense of the word), which means His body was wrapped in strips of cloths and spices to preserve it. According to John 19:39 the spices they used in this burial process weighed 75 pounds alone! Add in the cloth that was needed, and Jesus could have literally been encased in a 100-pound corpse cocoon.

Researchers tell us that the rocks that were usually rolled over these types of tombs would take 20 or so men to move.[3]

The reason? To prevent grave robbers from stealing stuff.

INSANE BRAIN STRAIN

Our whole faith rests on an event that many people would say is impossible: A man raised from the dead. How would you answer these critics?

In addition, to prevent the disciples from stealing the body and faking a "resurrection," the Jewish authorities convinced the Roman leaders to seal the tomb with a Roman seal and dispatch of at least four squads of soldiers to guard the tomb.

Now you have got to understand that Roman soldiers were the most highly trained, intensely disciplined soldiers on the planet. If they failed on their watch, it meant immediate execution. What happened to these tough guys on the morning of the Resurrection? They met somebody much tougher. Check this out:

> There was a violent earthquake, for an angel of the Lord came
> down from heaven and, going to the tomb, rolled back the stone
> and sat on it. His appearance was like lightning, and his clothes
> were white as snow. The guards were so afraid of him that they
> shook and became like dead men. (Matthew 28:2-4)

When they saw an angel of the Lord, these big, tough Roman soldiers had a panic attack—a seizure of biblical proportions—and passed out cold. Ha!

After Jesus rose from the dead He appeared to more than 500 people (1 Corinthians 15:6) over the course of 40 days (Acts 1:3). Many of these witnesses died for their testimony of the resurrection.[5] Now, sometimes people will die for what they think to be the truth, but nobody will die for what they know to be a lie!

Stop and think about this. If you were to line up these witnesses in a court of law and each of them were to be grilled on the stand for half an hour, you would have testimony from eyewitnesses of the resurrected Christ for more than 10 days straight.

Go Figure!

Open your Bible and read Acts 1:1-3, then answer these questions:

1. What are the "many convincing proofs" this verse is talking about?

_____

_____

_____

2. Why do you think Jesus stayed on earth 40 days after He came back from the dead?

_____

_____

_____

3. Why didn't He stay longer? Why didn't He stay forever?

_____

_____

_____

4. What impact does the Resurrection have on the claims Jesus made about Himself?

_____

_____

_____

5. Why do people refuse to believe in the Resurrection even though there are "many convincing proofs"?

_____

_____

_____

Think about it: Two or three solid eyewitnesses in a court of law are enough to convict or acquit somebody. What could over 500 rock-solid witnesses for the defense of the Resurrection do?

So What?

What does this all have to do with you and your life? Believe it or not, a whole stinking lot. You see, if Jesus rose from the dead, then He was who He claimed to be. And if He was who He claimed to be, then what He said was true. And if what He said was true, then your service to God matters.

The bottom line is this: If Jesus rose from the dead, then you need to serve the resurrected Christ with all your heart, soul, mind, and might. If He didn't rise from the dead, then go ahead and get drunk, plastered, buzzed, and all sexed up. Why? Because it doesn't matter.

Listen to the very blunt words of the apostle Paul in 1 Corinthians 15:14-19, 32:

> And if Christ has not been raised, our preaching is useless and so is your faith. More than that, we are then found to be false witnesses about God, for we have testified about God that he raised Christ from the dead. But he did not raise him if in fact the dead are not raised. For if the dead are not raised, then Christ has not been raised either. And if Christ has not been raised, your faith is futile; you are still in your sins. Then those also who have fallen asleep in Christ are lost. If only for this life we have hope in Christ, we are to be pitied more than all men. . . . If the dead are not raised,
>
> > "Let us eat and drink,
> > for tomorrow we die."

If Jesus didn't rise from the dead, then we are idiots for dedicating our lives to a dead man. If Jesus did rise from the dead, then every second we live on this planet has eternal ramifications. Why? Because someday we will stand before the resurrected Christ and give an account of our lives.

Bottom line: I believe He rose from the dead, not just because of the overwhelming witnesses who saw Him after the resurrection or the changed lives I see all around me. I believe, ultimately, simply because the Bible tells me so.

Do you?

YOU'RE NEXT!

Using what you learned from this chapter, take some time and write out an answer to the imaginary person who wrote this letter.

Dear Friend,

I'm turning to you because I think I've lost all hope. For years I have tried to fill my life with the things I thought would make me content and give me happiness, but now I realize there are not enough drugs, alcohol, sex, or money in the world to do that. So now I'm left with nothing, feeling nothing, but wanting everything. As I was thinking through my life, images of you kept coming up like a flashing light, like someone was trying to tell me something. All of a sudden it hit me. There is a piece to your life that I don't have. It's not that you're perfect or even happy all the time, but you have a peace and a hope that I can't get my fingers on. So I beg you, please tell me how you have managed to find something that seems to be drifting further and further away from me with each passing day . . .

Please tell me, before it's too late.

Signed,

Desperate

Dear Desperate,

_____

_____

_____

_____

_____

_____

_____

_____

_____

_____

_____

_____

Your friend

For more info on **The Big Q: How do I know Jesus really rose from the dead?** visit www.dare2share.org/soulfuel/archives and check out *Soul Fuel* question #5.

CHAPTER 9

Let Jesus into Your What?

Every week after the flannel-graph special-effects show, my Sunday school teacher challenged us kids to "let Jesus into our hearts."

As a neurotic little eight-year-old I had this mental picture of Jesus desperately trying to squeeze into each ventricle of my heart—all to no avail. Somehow I was blocking Him from coming into my heart with some subconscious brain impulse.

I must have asked Jesus to come into my heart a hundred times. I tried asking Jesus into my heart again and again and again. Was He there? I didn't know. My eight-year-old thought processes during these gospel presentations went something like this: "Jesus, please come into my heart. Are You there? Over? Can You knock three times on my pancreas if You made it in? If I get a heart transplant, will I lose my salvation? Just in case, Jesus, come into my heart again. Are You there yet? Over?"

These thoughts and more spun in my tiny, hyperactive brain every time I heard the phrase "let Jesus into your heart." But part of my problem was my Sunday school teacher's fault. She was unintentionally confusing me with a figurative term that I took literally.

I don't know exactly where this language came from. Some well-meaning preacher generations ago probably misread the Bible and coined a phrase that has confused a lot of children, teens, and even adults over the years. Don't get me wrong. I'm sure that tens of thousands of people have heard this same phrase and come to Christ as Savior. But for those of us who aren't quite as sharp, the whole "let Jesus into your heart" thing can be quite confusing.

That's why I thank God for Pastor Claude Pettit. On June 23, 1974, he clearly explained to me that eternal life is a free gift that we receive when we simply believe that Jesus died for us on the cross and trust in Him alone to forgive us for all of our sins. When Pastor Pettit explained this message to me, the confusion evaporated and the neuroses disappeared.

No longer did I think that going to heaven was a matter of confessing every sin I had ever committed or asking Jesus into my heart countless times until one of them took. I finally understood the gospel message: Jesus died for me and my sin. He paid the price for all my sins, so through simple faith in Him, and not in my good deeds or in my endless confessions or little prayers, I had eternal life.

In a flash I had confidence in Christ, and I knew I had eternal life. In that moment my life was transformed, my sins were forgiven, and, guess what? Jesus came to live in my heart! Jesus coming into my heart is a result of my faith according to Ephesians 3:16-17: "I pray that out of his glorious riches he may strengthen you with power through his Spirit in your inner being, **so that Christ may dwell in your hearts through faith.**"

✻ ✻ ✻

The Big Q: What is a Christian, and how does a person become one?

A Christian is someone who belongs to Jesus. How do we become a Christian? Believe it or not, it's much more simple than you may think. Don't take my word on that . . . take Jesus' word!

Here is what He tells us about how to receive eternal life:

For God so loved the world that he gave his one and only Son, that whoever believes in him shall not perish but have eternal life. (John 3:16)

✳ ✳ ✳

"I tell you the truth, whoever hears my word and believes him who sent me has eternal life and will not be condemned; he has crossed over from death to life." (John 5:24)

✳ ✳ ✳

"I tell you the truth, he who believes has everlasting life." (John 6:47)

If you simply believe in Christ, you have eternal life. That word *believe* doesn't just mean that you accept the fact He existed and died on a cross for your sins. It means to literally "trust, depend on, rely upon fully." This is the same kind of faith we exercise when we plop down on a chair and expect it to hold us up. If you trust in Jesus you are putting your full weight of dependence on Him and what He did for you on the cross.

This assumes you understand the following: (1) Doing good deeds is not good enough to get you into heaven. (2) Because you are human, you have already been poisoned by the sin of Adam and Eve, and God will never allow that toxic sin into His perfect kingdom. (3) Sin saturates your soul, and you should be condemned.

You can't cover up the fact that you are sinful, even if you live a "good" life. For example, let's say that I baked you a cake and burned it badly. If I were to cover it in white frosting and give it to you, the cake would still be burned even though you couldn't tell it from the outside. As soon as you bit into it, you would know. Putting white frosting on a burnt cake doesn't change the fact that the cake is ruined. Covering our sinful lives with good deeds doesn't change the fact that we have sinned. God sees right through the "frosting."

Go Figure!

Open your Bible to Ephesians 2:8-9, read the passage, and answer these questions:

1. According to this passage, what are we saved by and through?

   _____

   _____

   _____

2. When the word *gift* is used to describe our salvation (our deliverance from the penalty of sin), what does that imply?

   _____

   _____

   _____

3. If we could earn it through our good works, would it still be a "gift"?

   _____

   _____

   _____

4. Just because it is free, does that mean it's worthless? Why or why not?

   _____

   _____

   _____

5. Why do people try to "earn" salvation on their own?

_____

_____

_____

6. According to verse 9, if we could earn salvation, then what might we be tempted to do?

_____

_____

_____

Be warned! There are those out there who think that believing in Jesus is not enough! They believe you have to do something more. Whether it be going to church more, confessing more, reading your Bible more, surrendering yourself more, or whatever more, just remember that when you add to the gospel, it's like pouring poison in your bottle of water. It ruins it and will ruin those who ingest it!

Check out this serious warning in Galatians 1:8-9: "But even if we or an angel from heaven should preach a gospel other than the one we preached to you, let him be eternally condemned! As we have already said, so now I say again: If anybody is preaching to you a gospel other than what you accepted, let him be eternally condemned!"

The apostle Paul is declaring something pretty intense here! He is saying if you preach a different gospel message than the one he had been preaching, then you should be eternally condemned to hell. Wow! But Paul reemphasizes this by repeating it. Whenever the Bible says something once, you should stand up and salute. When it says it twice, then it's serious business.

INSANE BRAIN STRAIN

Since all your past, present, and future sins are completely forgiven the moment you trust Christ, what's the motivation to not sin anymore? Check out Paul's answer to this in Romans 6:1-14.

And what was the message that Paul was preaching? We see it clearly in Romans 4:5: "However, to the man who does not work but trusts God who justifies the wicked, his faith is credited as righteousness."

Notice in the phrase "to the man who does not work but trusts God" Paul is making it clear that becoming a Christian is not a matter of trying but trusting. So I have to ask you these questions, and I want you to answer them honestly in your mind right now:

Are you sure that you are a Christian?

Do you know that God wants a relationship with you?

But that your sins separate you from God?

That sins can't be removed by good deeds?

That Jesus paid the price for your sins, and everyone who trusts in Him is forgiven completely?

That you can have eternal life?

Do you know (I'm talking 100 percent sure) that you will go to heaven when you die?

If you could not honestly say yes to all these questions, I'm asking you to put your faith in Jesus right now. Trust in Him *alone* (more on that later) as your only hope of going to heaven, being rescued from hell, and having your sins eternally forgiven.

You can let God know this decision you are making by saying this simple prayer right now:

Dear God,

Right now I trust in Jesus to forgive all my sins, the ones that I committed in the past and the ones I will commit in the future. I have been poisoned by sin, and Jesus' death on the cross and resurrection provide the antidote. I know that I could never be good enough to make it into heaven. So I look to Jesus, the One who died for all my sins, and I trust in Him alone to give me eternal life. Thank You so much for this free gift.

In Jesus' name I pray,

Amen

Now let me make something perfectly clear: Saying a prayer never saved anyone from sin. Saying a prayer is simply a way of expressing to God that you are putting your faith in Jesus alone to save you from your sins and the penalty of your sins. There are many people who have "said the prayer" but never truly trusted in Jesus.

But if you have trusted in Jesus, you are a child of God forever! Welcome to the family of God! Now since He is Lord of your life, you can serve Him with all of your emotional, not literal, heart! Why? Not because you have to in order to go to heaven, but because you are thankful that you are!

BLAST FROM THE PAST

I once was lost, but now am found, was blind, but now I see.[1]

—John Newton, 19th century former slave trader

I still have the little red Bible I took to church the day I trusted Jesus. When we were leaving the church that momentous day over 30 years ago, I told my grandma that the gospel message finally made sense. Then she took my Bible and wrote these words: "On June 23, 1974, Greg Stier received Jesus Christ as his Savior."

I'm so thankful that Grandma did that. So I'm going to give you the opportunity to have that same privilege right now if you are trusting in Jesus for the first time.

"On _____ I, _____,
        (date/month/year)   (your name)

am trusting in Jesus alone to save me."

Now let somebody know this decision you made and let him or her celebrate with you.

If you were already a Christian when you started reading this chapter, remember to keep the gospel message simple and clear as you share it with others. Your friends who are as neurotic as I was (and still am) may not understand anything less than the simple gospel message.

So What?

This is the most important decision that faces every person on the planet. The decision to become or not become a Christian determines not only what your life is like here on earth, but what your life in eternity after death will be like as well. Because of this, it is critical that you make sure you are trusting in Christ alone as your only hope of salvation. There might be some of you reading this who are depending on the fact that you said some prayer or walked down front at a meeting to save you. It won't. God will not be mad at you for looking deep inside and making sure you are a Christian. Also, knowing how simple it is to become a Christian should take away the fear of telling your friends about how they can find eternal life.

YOU'RE NEXT!

Finish this poem:

> He died for me and ALL my sins,
>
> My new life in Him begins.
>
> I will live with Him in heaven's glory . . .

_____

For more info on **The Big Q: What is a Christian, and how does a person become one?** visit www.dare2share.org/soulfuel/archives and check out _Soul Fuel_ question #12.

CHAPTER 10

Bullets, Bibles, and the 'Burbs

My mom used to freak out all the time. She would tear the house apart looking for me. Had I run away? Was I deaf?

Yes. I had run away, and I was deaf. I had run away to the closet or underneath the bed or kitchen sink. And I had become deaf to everything and everyone around me. Why? Because I had discovered the Word of God and its power to change my life.

When Ma would finally look under the bed, open the closet door, or whip open the door under the kitchen sink, she would find me hunched over or stretched out with a flashlight and a Bible, totally oblivious to her screaming.

God's Word was an escape from my loud, superintense family. In the Bible's pages I found the Father I never knew. I found a kind of strength different from most of my family's. Instead of power that erupted from rippling biceps and triceps, the power I was discovering was spiritual.

Although I was raised in an area with one of the highest crime rates in Denver, and that violence was all around us, I had found a solace, a resting place in God and His Word.

By this time most of my family had come to Christ, but many of them were still pretty rough around the edges. That roughness definitely impacted my family's day-to-day approach to problem solving!

Like the time that the Harley guy who lived in the apartment above us cussed out my mom. Now Ma was tough, as I've already shared, but this guy was too big for even her to take out. So she made a call to newly converted Uncle Bob.

Bob must have been reading the Old Testament at the time because he drove right over, walked up the stairs, knocked on the guy's door, and, when the tough guy refused to apologize to my mom, "dealt" with him. This dealing included being thrown down a set of stairs, beaten pretty badly, and then told to pack and leave.

What's weird is that he did. I think he moved out that day.

And we were soon to follow. Ma had had enough of inner-city violence. This was the last straw. She packed up my brother and me and moved us to the suburbs of Denver. We moved into The Westminster Square Apartments. Although not the nicest part of town, it was a few notches safer than where we had been.

That's when we heard the news. The 20-something girl who had moved into our apartment after we left had been shot. Somebody knocked on the door, and when she looked through the peephole, she was shot. Thank the Lord that she survived this horrible shooting.

Years later I asked my mom, "Do you think that the person who shot that girl through the door was the Harley guy? Maybe he didn't know we moved. Maybe he thought he was shooting you when she looked through the peephole."

"You know, Greg," she said. "I've never put two and two together, but I bet you it was him."

We were spared from violence again. Weird. Strange. Divine.

Those three words pretty much sum up my life. But, as I've already made clear, what helped me survive the weirdness was the Word of God.

The Big Q: Is the Bible really God's Word, and does it really relate to my life?

The answer to both these questions is a big, fat YES! Here is what the Bible says about itself in 2 Timothy 3:16-17: "All Scripture is God-breathed and is useful for teaching, rebuking, correcting and training in righteousness, so that the man of God may be thoroughly equipped for every good work."

Notice what this passage is saying. First of all, it is reminding us that every word of Scripture (aka "The Bible") is breathed out by God. In a sense, talking is breathing out words. Those words go from your mouth to the ears of the one you are talking to. In the same kind of way, the words that God has breathed out are on the pages of the Bible and go to the eyes and then to the hearts of those who read it.

These words from God relate directly to our lives. They teach us how to live life, rebuke us when we mess up, correct us when we are off course, and train us how to live a life that is fully equipped for anything and everything.

This is one reason I love the Word of God so much, because as a kid, my life was filled with some raw, rough characters. Where did I turn for a moral compass to give me direction? The Bible. My life was turbulent, violent, and unsafe—crazy. Where did I go to learn how to lean on God for my sense of security and safety? The Bible.

 INSANE BRAIN STRAIN
How could 40 men, from three different continents, over the course of 1,500 years, write a book dealing with hundreds of subjects and never contradict each other once?

The answer to the mystery of this chaper's Insane Brain Strain is simple . . . it's a conspiracy! God conspired to speak His words to humanity in one compilation called the Bible, so He did something incredibly marvelous. He took full control of the writers through His Holy Spirit as they wrote. Check it out: "Above all, you must understand that no prophecy of Scripture came about by the prophet's own interpretation. For prophecy never had its origin in the will of man, but men spoke from God as they were carried along by the Holy Spirit" (2 Peter 1:20-21).

The Word of God was not made up in the minds of the writers of the Bible. Instead, these men were "carried along by the Holy Spirit" as they wrote. The whole idea of "carried along" back then was used to describe a ship in the ocean that had lost its rudder and was being "carried along" by the wind and the waves. It's the same phrase in Acts used to describe a ship that was getting battered by an intense storm. What does this mean when it comes to the writers of the Bible? The hurricane-strength force of the Holy Spirit took over the authors of the Bible as they were writing and drove every single part of the process. The result? Every word of the Bible, while still reflecting the personality of the human author, was ultimately from the divine author!

> **BLAST FROM THE PAST**
>
> The nature of water is soft, that of stone is hard; but if a bottle is hung above the stone, allowing the water to fall drop by drop, it wears away the stone. So it is with the Word of God; it is soft and our heart is hard, but the man who hears the Word of God often, opens his heart to the fear of God.[1]
>
> —ABBA POEMEN, 5TH CENTURY MONK

God's Word is full of God's words! And if they are God's words, they are perfect. "Every word of God is flawless" (Proverbs 30:5).

If God's Word was breathed out by God through men, then every word in it is flawless. Put another way, if there was a mistake in the words that the authors of the Bible penned, then there was a flaw in God. If God inspired every word, then every word emanates from who He is. A flaw in the original manuscripts would point to a flaw in the Originator of those manuscripts. But if every word was inspired by God (which I am convinced it was), then the Bible is the most perfect thing we have on planet earth!

How else do we know the Bible is the Word of God?

History supports it!

Because the New Testament provides the primary historical source for information on the resurrection, many critics during the nineteenth century attacked the reliability of these biblical documents. But according to Christian apologist Josh McDowell, "By the end of the 19th century, however, archaeological discoveries had confirmed the accuracy of the New Testament manuscripts."[2]

Prophecy proves it!

There are hundreds of precise prophecies in the Bible that have been literally fulfilled. Three hundred of them are specifically about Jesus Christ, and they all came true exactly as predicted! The odds of that happening have been estimated at 1 in 10^{17}. That's 1 in 100,000,000,000,000,000 chances! Can't visualize that number? Well, consider this illustration adapted from Josh McDowell:

> Imagine spreading iPods two feet deep across the entire state of Texas. Now imagine that I had engraved one of these iPods with the name Greg Stier. If I asked you to randomly pick out just one iPod from all the quadrillions of iPods spread out across all of Texas, your chances of pulling out mine on your first try would be 1 in 10 to the 17th power.[3]

Jesus said it!

Remember that the New Testament was not written until after Jesus rose from the dead. So when He refers to the Bible, He is speaking of the Old Testament—the Law and the Prophets. Here's what He said about them in Matthew 5:17-18:

> Do not think that I have come to abolish the Law or the
> Prophets; I have not come to abolish them but to fulfill them.
> I tell you the truth, until heaven and earth disappear, not the
> smallest letter, not the least stroke of a pen, will by any means
> disappear from the Law until everything is accomplished.

Jesus makes it very clear that the Old Testament is fulfilled in Him and will stay relevant until the end of time!

His resurrection seals it!

Think about it. If Jesus rose from the dead, then He was who He claimed to be. If He was who He claimed to be (which is God), then everything He said was true. Because again and again Jesus refers to the Bible and respects it as the very words of God, so we can do the same with absolute confidence!

Go Figure!

Read Psalm 19:7-11 and ask for God's insight as you answer these questions:

1. In verses 7 and 8 what are the four things that the Word of God can do for you?

   _____

   _____

2. How does God describe their worth in this passage?

_____

_____

_____

3. How should the Bible "taste" to us when we read it?

_____

_____

_____

4. How is reading/studying the Bible like eating something sweet?

_____

_____

_____

5. In verse 11 what are the results of God's Word in our lives?

_____

_____

_____

6. How has your personal reading of God's Word changed your life in the last two weeks?

_____

_____

_____

So What?

Think about it: On your shelf sit the very words of the all-powerful God of the universe. This is like getting a letter straight from heaven. So why then is it so tough to keep a regular schedule of reading the Bible? I think it's because most Christians don't truly grasp what it means to have God's Word at their fingertips. Would you open a letter you knew beyond the shadow of a doubt was from God? Of course you would! So why not commit right now to starting a regular Bible reading schedule? I guarantee your life will never be the same! Consider starting with the book of John or reading the chapter of Proverbs that goes with the day of the month (Proverbs 1 on the first day of the month, Proverbs 2 on the second . . . you get the picture). Allow God's Word to shape your character and choices as you live each day.

Maybe you don't want to read your Bible under a kitchen sink or in a closet. But I challenge you to pick a place to devour God's words daily. Let them radically change your life as they did mine!

YOU'RE NEXT!

Read Psalm 119:97-104 a few times, then rewrite this passage in your own words as a prayer to God. Here is an example taken from verses 101-104.

I have kept my feet from every evil path and decisions that go against Your Word so that I might obey Your Word.

Lord, I will really try to avoid . . .

_____

_____

_____

_____

_____

I have not departed from Your laws,
keep with me,
because they are straight from You!
For You Yourself have taught me.

The things I learn in the Bible will . . .

_____

_____

_____

_____

How sweet are Your words to my taste,
your Word than in any other hobby or habit
sweeter than honey to my mouth!

I will find more satisfaction and joy . . .

_____

_____

_____

_____

_____

I gain understanding from Your precepts;
how evil it is to sin against You;
therefore I hate every wrong path.

After reading Your Word, I understand . . .

_____

_____

_____

_____

✳ ✳ ✳

For more info on **The Big Q: Is the Bible really God's Word, and does it really relate to my life?** visit www.dare2share.org/soulfuel/ archives and check out *Soul Fuel* question #8.

CHAPTER 11

Death Encounter #3: Butterscotch Candy

It looked tasty—that orangey-yellowish disk, wrapped in the transparent wrapper. It was there just for me. Nobody was there to challenge my right to eat it. Ma was at work. My brother, Doug, was off at school or something. It was just me and it.

My plan was to unwrap that piece of butterscotch candy, pop that flying-saucer-shaped piece of confectionary delight into my mouth, and then suck on it for as long as I could. When I could stand it no longer (usually about one minute) I would bite my little piece of hard candy and crunch it into tiny pieces of mouth-tantalizing oblivion, savoring every phase of its yummy destruction. Its pain would be my gain.

But the plan went awry.

After successfully completing the unwrapping phase, I failed miserably at the pop-into-the-mouth phase. I popped it a little too far. It went right past my mouth and down, not my throat, but my windpipe.

I was in trouble. Not only could I not breathe, but I could not gasp or cough or anything. It was like someone took a pair of pliers and completely cut off my breathing tube. It's almost as though that piece of butterscotch candy had a vendetta and was determined to get the last laugh, refusing to be bested by a nine-year-old.

I couldn't call anybody because I couldn't talk. Even if I called 911 it would probably be several minutes before anyone got there, and by that time it would be too late. Starting to panic, I tried reaching down my throat, to no avail. I would have thrown my stomach onto a chair back had I known the Heimlich maneuver, but I didn't know it. The only thing I knew was that if I didn't do something quickly, I would die. With a dash I ran outside and banged furiously on the door to the apartment next to us. But nobody was home.

I stumbled out to the street to try to wave down any cars that just happened to be driving by, but our usually busy thoroughfare was dead silent . . . like I was soon to be. It's almost as though I could hear faint butterscotch-sounding laughs coming from my blocked throat. This evil little piece of candy was taunting me. It looked as if I wasn't going to crunch it into oblivion after all. It looked as if it was going to choke me all the way to the pearly gates.

I could feel myself losing consciousness. This was serious. I knew I was about to die. So I stopped running toward the street looking for cars to flag down. I stopped dead in my tracks and just prayed, *Save me, God! I am about to die! Please show me what to do!*

In the millisecond that followed it's *almost* as though I heard a voice say, "Stand on your head." I immediately put my head on the ground, put both of my hands palms-down on the dirt, and lifted my feet straight into the air.

That little butterscotch candy dislodged from my windpipe, gravity as its nemesis, and fell right into my mouth.

At first I stood up and spit that little candy devil into my hand, gasping for air and catching my breath. God had answered my prayer and spared my life once again.

In that moment, I thought about throwing that piece of candy to the dirt. But I refused to be bested. I placed the piece of candy carefully in my mouth (no more "popping" for me) and crunched it into candy heaven, or, hopefully, to confectionary hell.

Who saved me? God!

What saved me? Prayer!

In the midst of my rushing around trying to figure out a solution to my problem, it wasn't any of my solutions that worked. It was the solution that God gave me as the result of a simple prayer that saved me from death once again.

The Big Q: What is prayer, and how do I do it?

When I think of the word *prayer*, I think of that time I asked God for help with a piece of hard candy stuck in my windpipe.

There was nothing fancy about my prayer. I simply talked to God.

That's what prayer is, talking to God, letting Him know your thoughts, your dreams, your needs, and what you are thankful for. Think of prayer as a conversation that you would have with your closest friend, except in this case, your closest friend is the Maker and Master of the universe.

Jesus taught His disciples how to pray in Matthew 6:9-13:

> "This, then, is how you should pray:
> > "Our Father in heaven,
> > hallowed be your name,
> > your kingdom come, your will be done
> > on earth as it is in heaven.
> > Give us today our daily bread.
> > Forgive us our debts,

as we also have forgiven our debtors.
And lead us not into temptation,
but deliver us from the evil one."

Jesus does something significant in this passage. He gives His disciples a model prayer. We know it as the Lord's Prayer, but He gave it to the disciples, and since we are His disciples as well, we could really call this prayer our own.

This prayer was not designed to be a rote script, but a guide that we use as we pray. It is more of a compass than a map. It points us in the right direction as we talk to God. Let's take a closer look at five aspects of this prayer, phrase by phrase.

1. Praise: "Our Father in heaven, hallowed be your name"—This is like us, talking to God the Father in prayer, praising Him for who He is. When we "hallow" His name, we are simply recognizing His holiness, His greatness, His majesty.

So when's the last time you just praised God for who He is? When's the last time you boasted to God about God? Take some time and tell God how awesome you think He is right now. It's a good habit to include this in every prayer.

2. Priorities: "Your kingdom come, your will be done on earth as it is in heaven"—In this part of our prayer we are asking God to let His priorities rule, not ours. Ultimately this life, all life, is not about us—it's about Him and His purposes. It's about His establishing His kingdom on the earth someday. It's about everyone on this planet obeying His will fully, just as the angels in heaven do.

When's the last time you prayed for God's goals to be accomplished and not just your own? Too many times we utter purely self-centered prayers that are not about Him ruling this planet, but us running our world.

INSANE BRAIN STRAIN
The first two phrases of this prayer have nothing to do with us or our needs but God and His priorities. Why does God tell us to pray to Him about His priorities? Doesn't He already know them?

3. Provision: "Give us today our daily bread"—Prayer also includes asking God for the things that we need and want. While God will not always give us the things we want, He will ultimately always provide what we need. We may not understand it at the time, but looking back someday, we will realize that He provided all our needs and many of our wants. Why does He do this? Because He is a loving Father who wants to give us good things. Listen to the words of Jesus in Matthew 7:9-11:

> "Which of you, if his son asks for bread, will give him a stone? Or if he asks for a fish, will give him a snake? If you, then, though you are evil, know how to give good gifts to your children, how much more will your Father in heaven give good gifts to those who ask him!"

These good gifts aren't always what we originally asked for, but, in the long run, they are the best gifts. Ask God to provide. Let Him know the desires of your heart. Then trust in Him to give you what is best!

Are you boldly asking God to provide your needs? Do you really believe He will give you the best every time, even when it doesn't seem like it?

4. Pardon: "Forgive us our debts, as we also have forgiven our debtors"—Part of prayer involves asking God for forgiveness for those we have hurt or sinned against (including God) and choosing to forgive those who have hurt us. The Bible says that if we confess our sins to God, He will forgive us. This forgiveness is a different kind of forgiveness from the kind you receive at salvation. When you trust in Christ as your savior, you are legally and totally forgiven for all your sins in the courtroom of God. Those sins will never be held against you in an eternal sense.

But the kind of forgiveness that Jesus is referring to in His model prayer is the kind that keeps you out of hot water. In other words, for you God is no longer a Judge to be feared but a Father to be obeyed. The Judge that condemned you to hell before you were a believer adopted you into His own family at the moment you trusted in Jesus as your only hope of salvation. But if you disobey your heavenly Father, you will damage your relationship with Him. Your joy in God will be deflated, distance will creep into your relationship, and God's disci-

> **BLAST FROM THE PAST**
> There is not in the world a kind of life more sweet and delightful than that of a continual conversation with God.[1]
> —Brother Lawrence, 17th century Carmelite monk

pline will drop. So when you ask for forgiveness, you are not doing it to keep out of hell; you are doing it to keep open your relationship with Daddy! So confess your sins and believe that God will forgive you completely!

5. Protection: "And lead us not into temptation, but deliver us from the evil one"—Prayer includes asking God for protection from temptation from within and Satan's attacks from without. We ask God to help us walk His path through His strength and to deliver us from Satan's wicked grasp.

Sin and Satan are lurking in the shadows all around you. You can see their reflection in the computer screen in your room. You can hear their whisper in your friends' call to gossip about the latest rumors. You can feel their tug when your jealousy stirs or your selfish anger rises.

Pray for God to deliver you from evil and the evil one.

Go Figure!

Open your Bible and ask God to help you as you read James 5:16-18.

1. What is the relationship between confession of sin and prayer?

_____

_____

_____

2. What does it mean to be a "righteous" person?

_____

_____

_____

3. What is the relationship between righteousness and our prayers?

_____

_____

_____

4. Why does James use the words *powerful* and *effective*?

_____

_____

_____

5. Do you consider your prayers "powerful" and "effective"? Why or why not?

_____

_____

_____

6. Why does James use the example of Elijah?

_____

_____

_____

7. How does the fact that Elijah's prayers changed the weather affect your view of prayer?

_____

_____

_____

So What?

You have direct access to the God of the universe. If that doesn't blow your mind, I'm not sure what would. This is where the two-way communication comes in—God talks to you through His Word (the Bible), and then you respond. You can also talk to God anytime, anywhere, about anything. In fact, God wants you to talk to Him more than you do! He's never too busy to listen, which is one huge reason why we should never be too busy to talk to Him. Get the convo with God going today and make time to pray every day—and all your tomorrows will be radically changed.

Get in the habit of it to the point where you are praying spontaneously all the time, until it is as natural as breathing.

Speaking of breathing, I'm so glad that I still am. Anyway, I've got to go. I'm kind of in the mood for a snack. I know . . . butterscotch!

Note to self: Place, don't pop!

YOU'RE NEXT!

Read Matthew 6:9-13. Jesus' prayer is divided into phrases below. Next to each phrase, write down what it means to you, based on what you've learned from this chapter. Then pray through the prayer as it appears in your own words.

Jesus' Words	Your Words
Our Father in heaven,	_____
hallowed be your name,	_____
your kingdom come,	_____
your will be done	_____
on earth as it is in heaven.	_____
Give us today our daily bread.	_____
Forgive us our debts,	_____
as we also have forgiven our debtors.	_____
And lead us not into temptation,	_____
but deliver us from the evil one.	_____

For more info on **The Big Q: What is prayer, and how do I do it?** visit www.dare2share.org/soulfuel/archives and check out *Soul Fuel* question #25.

CHAPTER 12

Adam, Eve, and the Missing Link

Nobody likes going to a new school, especially in the middle of the school year. Friendships are already set, cliques are fully in place, and everyone is looking for the new kid to pick on.

I was the new kid, the city kid who moved to the suburbs. The transition from Brown Elementary to Vista Grande Elementary was not a smooth one.

Why?

Well, it wasn't just different kids in a different setting, but it was a totally different teaching philosophy. Brown was pretty traditional straight-up A-B-Cs, 1-2-3s, addition, subtraction, multiplication stuff. But Vista was one of those prototype elementary schools that was going to revolutionize education.

Right.

It was considered an "open" school where children took packets and completed them at their own pace. Teachers were there, not really as teachers, but as mentors and guides. Yeah, it all sounded good, but a hyperactive kid like me needed structure.

I think completing one of the science packets that I was "pacing" myself through was what sparked the original question. It was the question of evolution.

Now, I was a big dinosaur/Neanderthal man fan up to that point. I loved to play with my dinosaur toys and imagine what it must have been like to live back in those times. At the same time, I had always believed in the biblical story of Adam and Eve. To me the whole idea of Neanderthal men and Adam and Eve was not a conflict . . . until then.

I started sensing the conflict between believing both the biblical story of Adam and Eve and the idea of evolution and the missing link, a type of "man" that supposedly evolved from apes into humans. So I asked one of my teachers—er, excuse me, *guides*—about it. We'll call her Mrs. X. Here's the gist of the conversation:

GREG: Hey, Mrs. X, how are you?

MRS. X: Great, Greg. What's up?

GREG: I have a question about my science packet.

MRS. X: What is it?

GREG: Well, I was reading it, and it was talking about evolution and Neanderthal men and missing links and stuff and it hit me, if Adam and Eve were the first man and woman that God created, then where do Neanderthal men come from?

MRS. X: Um, well, Greg, evolution and the existence of Neanderthal men are scientific fact. The story of Adam and Eve, while a beautiful story, is just a wonderful fairy tale.

At that second I felt my first serious internal theological conflict. My little world had been shaken to its core, and I had to choose: Did I accept the "hard science" of atheistic evolution—that everything came about by random chance—or did I believe the "fairy tale" of Scripture, that God created everything, including me?

* * *

The Big Q: Did God create everything, and why does it matter?

That was a defining moment for me. For the next few minutes, I launched into my first serious defense of my faith. I told Mrs. X that, while I didn't understand all the facts, I did know this: If atheistic evolution was in conflict with the biblical account, I would side with Scripture.

That was the moment I became a creationist. It seemed to me that it took more faith to believe that this universe came into being as a result of random chance than it did that all of it was spoken into existence by a God who has always been. His name is "I AM," after all.

Now, it's at this point that a lot of Christian books go on and on about facts and stats that prove the superiority of creation science (often called Intelligent Design) over atheistic evolutionary theory. Those guys are much smarter than I. I'm not going to try to scientifically prove creation to you. Nor am I going to try to disprove evolution to you. To be honest, I'm not smart enough to do either.

In order to understand the Scriptures, however, you have to trust them. That's why when I read, "In the beginning God created the heavens and the earth" in Genesis 1:1, I believe it.

That's why when I read, "God saw all that he had made, and it was very good. And there was evening, and there was morning—the sixth day" in Genesis 1:31, I believe it.

And when I read in John 1:3, "Through him all things were made; without him nothing was made that has been made," I believe it.

And when I read in Colossians 1:15-16, "He is the image of the invisible God, the firstborn over all creation. For by him all things were created: things in heaven and on earth, visible and invisible, whether thrones or powers or rulers or authorities; all things were created by him and for him"—you guessed it. I believe it.

INSANE BRAIN STRAIN

Why is there so much controversy surrounding the phrase "in the beginning God created"?

For me, this argument is not about science or theories. It's about God's Word and whether or not we choose to believe He is the Creator. The apostle Paul took the Genesis account seriously, too. Adam was no character in a "fairy tale" to him. Paul says in Romans 5:19, "For just as through the disobedience of the one man the many were made sinners, so also through the obedience of the one man the many will be made righteous."

BLAST FROM THE PAST

After many years of intense study of the problem of origins from a scientific viewpoint, I am convinced that the facts of science declare special creation to be the only rational explanation of origins. "In the beginning God created . . ." is still the most up-to-date statement that can be made about our origins.[1]

—Dr. Duane T. Gish, 20th century biochemist

This passage makes it clear that Adam is crucial to the whole story of the gospel. It was the real sin of a literal Adam that caused the whole of humanity to be poisoned by sin. This sets everything up for Jesus to die and redeem God's creation. Without Adam and his original sin, why would we need Jesus and His awesome salvation? What would we need to be saved from? To Paul, the man Adam was as real as the God-man Jesus.

Now, having said that, I have friends, Christian friends, who believe in what's called "theistic evolution." They believe that God used the process of evolution to create the universe around them.

While I differ with them, they are still my friends. I don't think that this is an issue we should divide over. Rather, it's an issue we should come together on and talk about, even debate about, in love. Just don't mistakenly think that you need a huge knowledge of science to understand the essential point of Genesis 1–2: God created the universe, and the most significant event in the whole process was when He created humans in His own image.

By the way, the whole idea of God creating the universe really gets me pumped up! Why? Because it shows me how truly powerful and awesome God is! If He can create everything out of nothing, then He can surely do anything! He didn't need time to be on His side, for He was the creator of time itself. He didn't need a random process to create, for He is the Creator!

Go Figure!

Open your Bible and ask God for help as you read Hebrews 11:1-13. Answer these questions:

1. How does "being sure of what we hope for and certain of what we do not see" apply to the origins debate?

   _____

   _____

   _____

2. Which does God commend people for—great scientific knowledge or great spiritual faith?

   _____

   _____

   _____

3. Why does it take faith to understand that "the universe was formed at God's command"?

_____

_____

_____

4. Does the phrase "the universe was formed at God's command" sound more like it is supporting creation or evolution? Why?

_____

_____

_____

5. Do both evolution and creation require some level of faith? Why or why not?

_____

_____

_____

So What?

Some of you may feel that same conflict in your soul right now as you read these words, the same conflict I felt when talking to Mrs. X. The question is whom are you going to side with: Adam and Eve or the Neanderthals?

Why does all this matter?

Simply this: God loves humans and He created them in His own image. People matter greatly to God. You matter greatly to God. You are His special creation—a creation so significant that God sent His only Son to die so that you can be in right relationship with Him. That has been His desire for you since the beginning.

And, as for the missing link, I believe the whole chain is gone! Sorry, Mrs. X!

YOU'RE NEXT!

Take some time and write out your thoughts about how the two different perspectives on the origin of life make you feel. Here's something to help you get started:

If God was not involved in the creation of life, this makes me feel _____, because _____.

If God created everything and all people are made in God's image, this makes me feel _____, because _____.

_____

_____

_____

_____

_____

_____

_____

Take a moment and say this prayer of thanksgiving to God for creating you in His image:

God,

I thank You that the beauty of Your creation surrounds me every day. I am amazed that You intricately designed me and created me in Your image! Thank You that Your creation serves as a continual reminder to me of Your awesome power and incredible love for me. Amen.

✳ ✳ ✳

For more info on **The Big Q: Did God create everything, and why does it matter?** visit www.dare2share.org/soulfuel/archives and check out *Soul Fuel* question #29.

CHAPTER 13

Who's Your Daddy?

Decades ago there was a young man named Tony, a religious man who came from a family with several ministers. One day he joined the army to fight for his country in the Korean War.

In many ways, he felt like he had found his calling. Why? Because he was an excellent soldier. During one bloody battle with the North Koreans, he was captured by his enemies, imprisoned, and tortured. But he never gave up hope, and he survived the years of torture. The North Koreans finally released him a full three years after the war was over. Upon coming back to America, he was decorated as a war hero.

Tony had proven himself on the battlefield, but in the battle for his own faith he was losing. After returning to the States, his spiritual life took a turn for the worse. He began to drift into a life of sin.

His Bible was replaced with a bottle. He began to pursue a lifestyle that was contrary to his religious upbringing. As the years passed, he went from marriage to marriage and relationship to relationship.

One day Tony's sister introduced him to her friend Shirley. They partied. She got pregnant.

When he found out she was pregnant, he left town.

A few years later, Tony died. Among the things he had left to show for his life were an old, dusty Bible he used to preach from, a

few tarnished medals from the war, and a son he had never met . . .
me. The only other thing I really know about my dad is he abandoned me and my mom before I was even born. But please hold the
pity. I have another Daddy who will never abandon me, who will
never cut and run.

So if my earthly dad left us, how did I discover all this stuff? The
same way I found out that Ma had almost aborted me. Someone flat-
out told me. This fateful night I was around 12 years old, and Ma
brought me to meet the woman who introduced her to Tony. The
woman was Tony's sister, my aunt.

Over the course of a few hours, she filled me in on Tony's life.

Learning more about my dad
somehow made his abandonment of
me feel more personal, and it took
me years to forgive him. But in the
long run, knowing more about my
dad was a good thing. Because since
then, I have discovered two more sis-
ters and a brother from Tony's marriages—siblings I never knew I had.

> **BLAST FROM THE PAST**
>
> Upon you I call, O God, my mercy, who
> made me and did not forget me when I
> forgot you.[1]
>
> —SAINT AUGUSTINE, 4TH CENTURY BISHOP

What does all this have to do with you? Just as I had another
entire human family I wasn't aware of, you have a whole spiritual
family you may not be aware of. You have a Dad who will never leave
you or forsake you! You have a spiritual family of brothers and sisters
with whom you are going to spend an eternity.

As you read this, you may feel wounded or abandoned by a mom
or a dad or a friend who let you down in a big way. If not, then prepare yourself. It's almost a sure thing that in coming months and
years, somebody close to you will turn their back on you. Even Jesus'
friends abandoned Him for a time.

It's during these periods when we often become aware of the

presence of our heavenly Daddy. We experience His all-encompassing, never-ending love, which leads us to the question . . .

The Big Q: Will God ever leave or forsake me?

Here's God's answer to that question in Hebrews 13:5: "Never will I leave you; never will I forsake you."

Now, in the original language the New Testament was written in, Koine Greek, there are five negatives in this passage. In a powerful and personal way God is telling us through this verse, "I will *never, never, never, never, never* leave you or forsake you."

Every time you doubt if God still loves you or think that He might abandon you for what you've done, make a fist. That's right, make a fist and hold it up to your face and say this out loud:

> "I will *never,*" then hold up your thumb.
> *"never,"* index finger up
> *"never,"* middle finger up
> *"never,"* ring finger up
> *"never,"* pinkie finger up
> "leave you or forsake you."

Then look at all your outspread fingers for a while and contemplate His commitment to you no matter what.

Go Figure!

Ask for God's insight as you read Romans 8:31-39 and answer these questions:

1. Why can't anyone, including Satan, bring a charge against us that sticks?

_____

_____

_____

_____

2. What is Jesus doing for us right now in heaven?

_____

_____

_____

_____

3. What does it mean to be "more than a conqueror"?

_____

_____

_____

_____

4. Is there anything in this universe (including yourself) that could separate you from God's love?

_____

_____

_____

_____

5. Even though sometimes you feel as if God isn't near, does that mean it's true? Why or why not?

_____

_____

_____

_____

6. Knowing that you could never escape the love of God, what are you willing to do to show Him your love for Him?

_____

_____

_____

Here are a few other verses to think about when you are worried that God may forsake you or abandon you:

"All that the Father gives me will come to me, and whoever comes to me I will never drive away. For I have come down from heaven not to do my will but to do the will of him who sent me. And this is the will of him who sent me, that I shall lose none of all that he has given me, but raise them up at the last day." (John 6:37-39)

* * *

"I give them eternal life, and they shall never perish; no one can snatch them out of my hand." (John 10:28)

* * *

He who began a good work in you will carry it on to completion until the day of Christ Jesus. (Philippians 1:6)

So What?

How does all of this apply to you? If you have put your faith and trust in Jesus alone to forgive you for all your sins, you are a child of God. You can be confident that your relationship with God is personal and permanent. This confidence is a reason to serve God, not a license to sin against Him.

Now let me ask you the million-dollar question: If I were to give you a million dollars right now, would you slap me and walk away? I don't think so. Why? Because you would be grateful for my free gift. As a matter of fact, if right after that I told you I was hungry, you would not hesitate to take me for a nice steak dinner. And if I needed a ride somewhere, you'd give me one gladly. Why? Because you are thankful!

 ## INSANE BRAIN STRAIN

If God can't tolerate or even look at sin, why doesn't He leave or forsake us when we sin?

A similar thing happens the moment you put your faith in Jesus. God gives you something infinitely more valuable than a million dollars. He gives you eternal life! Are you going to slap Him in the face and walk away, or are you going to serve Him? Of course you are going to serve Him! Why? Because you are grateful for His tremendous gift of eternal life!

It's at this point our minds can race to all sorts of different what-if scenarios. What if I do something really bad? What if I die right after I sin? What if . . . whatever.

I believe the only what-if you should be worried about is this one: What if you never truly believed in Jesus?

Here's how the Bible answers that one: "Examine yourselves to see whether you are in the faith; test yourselves. Do you not realize that Christ Jesus is in you—unless, of course, you fail the test?" (2 Corinthians 13:5).

So I ask you the question: "Are you sure that at some point in your life you have put your faith in Jesus alone to save you from your sins?"

If the answer is no, do it now (read chapter 9 again for help with that!).

If the answer is yes, then be confident in your relationship with God and live like you believe it. Inside everyone is a God-shaped hole that can only be filled by . . . well, God! The problem is that most people, even Christians, try to fill that hole with other things such as possessions, pleasure, and power. None of those things will ever work. Only our heavenly Daddy, who will never leave us or forsake us, can fill the void that makes life feel so empty and lonely. Because you know He is never going anywhere, you should put your complete trust in Him to meet all your needs. And especially when life feels like it couldn't get any more lonely, turn to your Father, who is right there waiting for you with open arms. Then serve Him with all your heart, soul, mind, and might. Why?

Because He will *never* (thumb), *never* (finger), *never* (finger), *never* (finger), *never* (pinkie) leave you or forsake you! Now give yourself a high-five!

Okay, don't.

Just know this: Although you may feel hurt or abandoned by your earthly family or friends, your heavenly Dad will always be there for you . . . always!

YOU'RE NEXT!

Read through the following prayer and mentally fill in the empty spaces with areas of personal struggle. Then pray this prayer of confession and thanksgiving to your heavenly Daddy who will never leave you or forsake you. (Use a separate piece of paper if you want to keep this private.)

Even though I have had thoughts like _____, You will never leave me.
Even though I have committed sins like _____, You will never leave me.
Even though I have said things like _____, You will never leave me.
Even though I have had feelings like _____, You will never leave me.

Dear heavenly Daddy,
Thank You for forgiving me and for Your promise that You will never, ever leave or forsake me.

✳ ✳ ✳

For more info on **The Big Q: Will God ever leave or forsake me?** visit www.dare2share.org/soulfuel/archives and check out *Soul Fuel* question #19.

CHAPTER 14

Yankee's Weird, Wild, and Wonderful Church

Remember Yankee? He was the fearless preacher who walked up to my uncle Jack's front door and boldly shared the gospel message with him. Over a period of two to three years, Yankee led many of my family members to Jesus. So when we moved to the suburbs of Denver, I started going to the church where he was a pastor, Colorado Bible Church.

Yankee's church was truly weird, wild, and wonderful. While it was not a superbig church (I think there were two to three hundred adults on a typical Sunday morning), the youth ministry was packed and stacked, wall to wall and floor to ceiling.

Yankee preached the gospel to anybody and everybody who would listen, but he had a special place in his heart for teenagers. For a while the youth ministry was averaging around 500 per week, and at one time it surged to more than 800 teenagers!

Don't ask me why, but for some reason Yankee was determined to call his youth ministry "Youth Ranch." It sounded like a juvenile detention center for naughty cowboys. Although I was only 11, some of my older friends snuck me in the first time I went. Here I was, a fifth-grader, in the middle of this loud crowd of teenagers who were singing about God and listening to God's Word.

A few things were special about Youth Ranch, and I noticed them during my first few visits. First of all, someone gave the gospel every week, and every week people would trust in Christ. I thought that was awesome.

The next thing I noticed was how clearly the gospel was presented (e.g., there was no "let Jesus into your what?" stuff). Yankee preached straight Jesus-on-the-cross/faith-alone gospel truth. Yankee sure knew how to make this gospel message simple and easy to understand, even for a crowd of rowdy, hormone-filled teenagers.

Another aspect of Yankee's youth ministry that stood out was that he would do anything, I mean *anything*, to get unreached teenagers to come and visit. We had 100-foot banana split nights. We had game nights. We had pie-eating contests. One time he gave away this sweet, red 1969 Firebird to the teen who brought out the most teenagers over the course of a

> **BLAST FROM THE PAST**
>
> The Lord showed me, so that I did see clearly, that he did not dwell in these temples which men had commanded and set up, but in people's hearts. . . . [H]is people were his temple, and he dwelt in them.[1]
>
> —George Fox, 17th century founder of the Quakers

few months. In one way it was all kind of cheesy. But in another way it showed Yankee was willing to do anything, even give away a car, so more teens would hear about Jesus.

But there was another part of the Youth Ranch experience that caught my attention. It was that everybody had a job to do. If you had attended Youth Ranch for more than two weeks in a row you got involved—period.

Whether it be handing out music books and Bibles, playing in the house band, welcoming first-time guests, or sitting with some-body you didn't know, everybody had a job to do.

In no time I got sucked up into the Youth Ranch experience. When I went there, I felt like I had a purpose, a mission, and a job to do.

Isn't that what church should be like for everyone? Instead, too many times, it is a place to go, sit, listen, pay, and then leave. But real church is a team game, not a spectator sport.

The Big Q: What is the church, and why should I be involved?

Before we take a look at what the church is, let's take a look at what the church is *not*. The church is not a building.

Now this may come as a surprise to you, but guess how many church buildings Christians owned in the early New Testament? None! They would borrow or rent buildings from time to time. But most of the time these early believers met in houses.

While there is nothing wrong with a church owning its own building, too many times churches today put more emphasis on a building rather than on the people who meet in it and live outside it. An immaculate lawn and spotless building should not be more important than a changed life and transformed community.

So what is the church? The word *church* comes from the Greek word *ecclesia*—which actually means "a gathering or assembly." It's when the people of God gather together to focus on Jesus. In Acts 2:42-47 we see what the first official church meetings were like. The basic elements of these original meetings help us understand what church should be like today.

They devoted themselves to the apostles' teaching and to the fellowship, to the breaking of bread and to prayer. Everyone was filled with awe, and many wonders and miraculous signs were done by the apostles. All the believers were together and had everything in common. Selling their possessions and goods, they gave to anyone as he had need. Every day they continued to meet together in the temple courts. They broke bread in their homes and ate together with glad and sincere hearts, praising God and enjoying the favor of all the people. And the Lord added to their number daily those who were being saved.

Go Figure!

Reread Acts 2:42-47 and answer these questions:

1. What four things did the early church devote itself to?

   _____

   _____

   _____

2. How did the people feel about going to church?

   _____

   _____

   _____

3. Why do you think they were filled with "awe"?

   _____

   _____

   _____

4. Describe the selflessness of these early Christians. When is the last time you saw that kind of attitude in your church?

_____

_____

_____

5. What is the ultimate result of their positive attitude and love for each other?

_____

_____

_____

6. How can you begin to bring this attitude and excitement into your church and youth group?

_____

_____

_____

Another term used in the Bible to describe the church is "the body of Christ." God uses this analogy to describe the importance of every part of the body of Christ. You are one of these parts. Read the following verses slowly and carefully:

The body is a unit, though it is made up of many parts; and though all its parts are many, they form one body. So it is with Christ. For we were all baptized by one Spirit into one body—whether Jews or Greeks, slave or free—and we were all given the one Spirit to drink.

Now the body is not made up of one part but of many. If the

foot should say, "Because I am not a hand, I do not belong to the body," it would not for that reason cease to be part of the body. And if the ear should say, "Because I am not an eye, I do not belong to the body," it would not for that reason cease to be part of the body. If the whole body were an eye, where would the sense of hearing be? If the whole body were an ear, where would the sense of smell be? But in fact God has arranged the parts in the body, every one of them, just as he wanted them to be. If they were all one part, where would the body be? As it is, there are many parts, but one body.

The eye cannot say to the hand, "I don't need you!" And the head cannot say to the feet, "I don't need you!" On the contrary, those parts of the body that seem to be weaker are indispensable, and the parts that we think are less honorable we treat with special honor. And the parts that are unpresentable are treated with special modesty, while our presentable parts need no special treatment. But God has combined the members of the body and has given greater honor to the parts that lacked it, so that there should be no division in the body, but that its parts should have equal concern for each other. If one part suffers, every part suffers with it; if one part is honored, every part rejoices with it.

Now you are the body of Christ, and each one of you is a part of it. (1 Corinthians 12:12-27)

I love this passage because it clarifies why you should be involved in your church and youth group. You are an essential part of the body of Jesus! Now, you may be thinking, *Well, I'm not so special. I can't speak in public. I can't sing or play in the worship band. What can I do?* But this passage makes it clear, "On the contrary, those parts of the body that seem to be weaker are indispensable." Do you know what this is saying? It's saying that your church and youth group can't run on all cylinders without you. Why? Because *you* are one of the cylinders!

And it is absolutely essential that your church and youth group are running on all cylinders. Why? Because the church is God's instrument of transformation on this earth!

INSANE BRAIN STRAIN

If the church is the "body of Christ," why are there so many different groups and denominations within one body?

Jesus said in Matthew 16:18, "I will build my church, and the gates of Hades will not overcome it." Jesus is actively building His church and using it as a battering ram against the gates of hell. You and I are literally big, whopping weapons in the hands of Jesus. He is using us to shatter the kingdom of darkness and plunder lost souls from the devil's dungeons of sin.

So What?

It's hard for me to imagine someone being a Christian and never getting involved in a church. It's not that going to church saves you, but if you're saved, you will want to go to church and get involved, because you are an essential part of the body. If you have no desire whatsoever to plug in to the body of Christ, you need to ask yourself why and start going to a church or youth group near you right away. If you're not involved in the church, there is a missing piece of your life that you'll want to fill. Figure out how you can help the church "run on all cylinders."

Does that sound exciting? Trust me, it is!

Thanks, Yankee, for showing me that the church is not about a building, but about the body of Christ on a mission from God to shatter the kingdom of Satan.

YOU'RE NEXT!

Write out a plan for the next few weeks or months about how you intend to get involved in your church. Here's an example to get you started.

This week I will call my youth leader and set up a time to meet and talk about how I can get involved. Time: _____ Place: _____

This month I will pray about how God wants me involved in helping the church do its job. Possible places of involvement:

Music

Drama

Welcoming

Outreach

Discipleship

_____

_____

_____

_____

_____

_____

_____

_____

_____

This month I will figure out how I can faithfully attend youth group every week so it can "run on all cylinders." Things I may need to cut back on (e.g., Facebook, work hours, sports, television):

_____

_____

_____

_____

_____

_____

* * *

For more info on **The Big Q: What is the church, and why should I be involved?** visit www.dare2share.org/soulfuel/archives and check out *Soul Fuel* question #22.

CHAPTER 15

$50 Worth of Pennies Buys a Lot

My family was pretty poor when I was growing up. Don't get me wrong. We always had food on the table. And whether it be the low income apartments, the dingy rental house, or the trailer (not a double-wide, mind you), we always had a roof over our heads. But other than the food and a roof, there wasn't much I could count on having. We lived simple lives.

In a one-month period robbers broke into our apartment twice during the day. The first time I walked in and saw the evidence of their forced entry through a window. A chill snaked down my back. The thieves could still be inside, and I didn't want to get shot.

As I walked through our ransacked apartment, I noticed something that disturbed me even more. Although they had torn the place apart looking for valuables, they hadn't actually stolen anything. And personally, I was offended. I had left my perfectly good Timex watch on the dresser, and they passed it by . . . thieves!

Let that be evidence we didn't have a lot of extra spending money. Even a penny amounted to something, so as far back as I can remember, I saved them. I would dig through the couch cushions, look under the car seats, ask family members for extra pennies, anything and everything to save them up. And save them I did.

By the time I was eight years old or so, I had saved $50 worth of pennies. I thought I was the richest kid in the world.

I'll never forget the day when Ma, her head bowed in humiliation, asked me if she could borrow my $50 in pennies for groceries. Of course I said yes, but I didn't forget the bill she "owed" me. I write with sarcasm because my mom worked her tail off providing for my brother and me. She left early and came home late. She was usually exhausted because she was a hard worker. And in the culture she worked in, the hardest workers got the hardest jobs, which made her even more tired. It took everything in my mom to ask me if she could borrow that money. She was a proud woman who had refused government assistance and was determined to raise us boys on her own.

Every once in a while I would remind my mom about the $50 debt, and she would say, "Don't worry, Son. I'm going to pay you back." But, as is so often the case, days turn to weeks, weeks to months, and months to years, and debts are forgotten.

Three years later Yankee decided that Colorado Bible Church was going to start a Christian school. Betty, Yankee's wife, told me about this Christian school and asked me if I wanted to attend.

I did. By this time I knew that I wanted to know the Bible as well as I possibly could. My 11-year-old mind, however, needed more than it could do on its own. I wanted teachers who would help me dive deeply into Scripture and master it.

The problem was the school's tuition cost $1,000 per year. While that may not sound like a lot of money to you, it might as well have been a million to us. When I brought up the Christian school to my mom, she said, "Honey, we just can't afford it."

A thought suddenly sprang to my mind, and so I pulled it out and threw it on the table, hoping it was my ace card in this game of parent poker.

"Ma," I said, "remember that $50 you borrowed from me for groceries three years ago?"

"Yes," she said quietly.

"Well, if you send me to Christian school, you don't have to pay me back."

I wasn't trying to manipulate my mom. I honestly thought it would help her to know the $50 invoice was cancelled. I hadn't put together how out-of-the-park $1,000 a year tuition was.

In her soul something happened. I witnessed it firsthand. Her head was down for a long time, and she looked up and stared me straight in my eyes and said, "I will find a way to send you there." As I looked in her eyes, I think I saw a tear. But she turned away before I could be sure.

Fifty dollars buys a lot.

It bought me a solid education at a Christian school that I loved.

It bought me the opportunity to study the Bible on an in-depth level.

It bought me the privilege of mastering theology even as a fifth-grader.

Come to think of it, it wasn't the $50 that bought anything. It was a mother's love.

* * *

The Big Q: Why should I study the Bible, and how do I do it?

This question was one of the driving reasons I wanted so badly to go to Arvada Christian School (ACS). I wanted to learn how to study the Bible.

To be honest, I already knew why I should study it. The transformed lives of my uncles Bob and Jack were reason enough for me.

And the changes I had felt in my own heart in my bumbling, fumbling attempts at Bible study convinced me that I needed to know more. It was at ACS that I hoped to learn it.

And learn it I did.

From the time I started at Arvada Christian School in fifth grade (with only 19 students total; that's right, *total*) the teachers started equipping us to study the Bible and apply its principles and lessons to our lives. We memorized verses in every class, even math. There were times I was memorizing entire books of the Bible as part of my projects.

But we didn't only memorize it; we were taught how to study it on our own.

I'll never forget when Mr. Ken Sanchez taught us how to study the Bible and understand the meaning of a text. He told us that he wanted us to go home that night and bring back something like 20 insights from John 3:16. Then he made us do it again the next night, with the same verse! And again the next night. And again. And again.

 ## INSANE BRAIN STRAIN

If we really believe that the Bible contains the words of God that have the power to transform our lives, why do we have such a hard time reading it and studying it?

Every day we came back with a list of fresh insights. Mr. Sanchez was making his point. What was it? That every book in the Bible is a bottomless well of truth and insight. The bucket that we use to draw out those insights is filled with these questions:

Who? What? When? Where? Why? and How?

Who wrote the verse? Who was it written to?

What does the verse mean? What does each of the phrases and words mean?

When was it written?

Where was it written from? Where were the recipients from?

Why was it written?

How does this all apply to me?

I guarantee you that if you apply these questions to every text of Scripture you study, you will get a lot more out of it. You will, with the help of the Holy Spirit who dwells inside every believer, be able to draw out the meaning for yourself.

But, to be honest, that's a lot of questions to ask every time you read the Bible. So I've developed my own streamlined edition of questions to ask: **"What?"** and **"So what?"**

What does this passage mean? To answer this question, you may have to ask some of the other questions listed above. You may have to read the verse again and again. You may have to read the verses around that verse to make sure you are reading it in what's called "the right context." You'll definitely have to pray and ask God, through His Holy Spirit, to make the meaning clear to you.

Second Timothy 2:15 is a powerful reminder. "Do your best to present yourself to God as one approved, a workman who does not need to be ashamed and who correctly handles the word of truth."

If we want to be an approved, unashamed ambassador of God, then we need to learn how to *correctly handle* God's Word. What does that mean? It means that we use it properly by doing our best to interpret it accurately. We don't make it say what we want it to say. Instead, we discover the meaning of the verse through prayer and study.

To go a little deeper on a particular subject there are a few tools you can get and use:

Bible concordance—this is a book that has every word in the Bible listed in alphabetical order and identifies where they occur. It's a great tool for looking up where different words and concepts are found in the Bible.

Bible dictionary—this is like an ordinary dictionary, except the words listed are taken only from the Bible.

Bible commentaries—these books help explain what verses, chapters, and books of the Bible mean and how they apply to life.

Study Bible—there are many study Bibles available that have built-in concordances, commentaries, and even dictionaries.

Bible software—check into Bible software that contains all of the above, and more.

Recommended Web sites: www.biblegateway.com, www.bible.org, and bible.crosswalk.com.

These resources will help you if you want to go deeper into a passage to discover its meaning. These books and Web sites, once you learn to navigate them, can be a tremendous help to you as you seek to understand the truths in the Bible.

But once you know the basic meaning of the verse or verses, you ask the next incredibly important question: So what?

So what does this mean for me?

In other words, how is the truth of this passage going to change my life today? Why is the "so what?" question important? Because in the book of James, God tells us that we should "be doers of the word and not hearers only."

Jesus tells a powerful story about why we should put into practice what we learn in the Bible:

> Therefore everyone who hears these words of mine and puts
> them into practice is like a wise man who built his house on the

BLAST FROM THE PAST

Make knowledge of the Scripture your love. . . . Live with them, meditate on them, make them the sole object of your knowledge and inquiries.[1]

—Saint Jerome, 4th century scholar

rock. The rain came down, the streams rose, and the winds blew and beat against that house; yet it did not fall, because it had its foundation on the rock. But everyone who hears these words of mine and does not put them into practice is like a foolish man who built his house on sand. The rain came down, the streams rose, and the winds blew and beat against that house, and it fell with a great crash. (Matthew 7:24-27)

I don't know if you've been noticing the "Go Figure!" section featured throughout this book, but this is one of the reasons for it. My goal is for this section to help you begin to ask and answer the right questions every time you open your Bible to read. As a matter of fact, you have a chance to do that in the "Go Figure!" section of this chapter! Go figure!

Be like a detective when you come to the Bible. Don't just read and read. Read and stop and think. Try to understand everything you read. For the verses that you don't get, keep studying and praying until God gives you the answer. Don't give up until you know **What?** and **So what?**

Go Figure!

Open your Bible and ask for God's help as you re-read Matthew 7:24-27. Answer the following questions:

1. How is reading and applying the Bible like building a house?

   _____

   _____

   _____

2. Do most Christians put God's Word into practice? Why or why not?

_____

_____

_____

3. How is hearing/reading God's Word but not applying it like building your life on sand?

_____

_____

_____

4. What do you think Jesus had in mind when He described rain and wind?

_____

_____

_____

5. How would applying the Bible help protect us from life's storms?

_____

_____

_____

6. What potential "crashes" could happen in your life if you don't start reading and applying the Bible to your life?

_____

_____

_____

Believe me. It's worth it. At the end of all your studies and your attempts at putting what you learn into practice is Jesus Himself. Through Scripture, you can better know Jesus personally and intimately.

So What?

In chapter 10, I encouraged you to start reading the Bible on a regular basis. Now it's time to take that reading to the next level by digging deeper! Reading the Bible is good, but studying it the way I've described is much better! Get a notebook and pen, check out those study tools, and begin an adventure that will last a lifetime. Remember, the Bible is the deepest book on planet earth; you can never dig so deep that you exhaust what you can learn. In fact, the deeper you go, the better diamonds you will find! Be sure to go to www.dare2 share.org and join one of our many message board discussions to share what you are learning, ask questions, and grow deeper in your faith.

It's weird, but in a lot of ways this book you're reading is the end result of my Christian school education. I'm passing on to you the lessons I learned there. If tens of thousands of teenagers buy this book (which I hope they will), then tens of thousands of teenagers will be directly impacted by the truths I learned at Arvada Christian School.

Yeah, $50 will buy a lot.

Thanks, Ma!

YOU'RE NEXT!

Write out a list of "storms" (see Matthew 7:24-27) that you have gone through or are going through right now. Note how they have affected or are affecting you. After you complete the list, go back and find Bible passages that could have helped you or could help you now in those situations and write them down. How can you find Bible passages that deal with the storms you are battling through? You could use a concordance, ask your youth leader, or look on the Internet for "Bible verses about _____," (you fill in the blank). Here are some general examples.

Storm #1—My Parents' Divorce

This storm made me feel like I was being abandoned and not loved anymore. I felt like I was being torn in two and left totally alone.

Psalm 23

The Lord is my shepherd, I shall not be in want.
He makes me lie down in green pastures,
he leads me beside quiet waters,
he restores my soul.
He guides me in paths of righteousness
for his name's sake.
Even though I walk
through the valley of the shadow of death,
I will fear no evil,
for you are with me;
your rod and your staff,
they comfort me.
You prepare a table before me
in the presence of my enemies.
You anoint my head with oil;
my cup overflows.
Surely goodness and love will follow me
all the days of my life,
and I will dwell in the house of the Lord
forever.

Storm #2—My Self-Image

I feel such pressure to look like the "beautiful" people on magazines and in movies, but there is no way. I'm not pretty or handsome, and I'm a little overweight. I feel so ugly!

Psalm 139:13-14

For you created my inmost being;
you knit me together in my mother's womb.
I praise you because I am fearfully and wonderfully made;
your works are wonderful,
I know that full well.

_____

_____

_____

_____

_____

_____

_____

_____

_____

* * *

For more info on **The Big Q: Why should I study the Bible, and how do I do it?** visit www.dare2share.org/soulfuel/archives and check out *Soul Fuel* question #26.

Grandpa, Ma, and her new husband on their wedding day.
Doesn't Grandpa look as if he just stepped off the set of a Mafia movie?

CHAPTER 16

Report Cards on Judgment Day

Grandpa's family emigrated from Wales, and he was the only one of his siblings born in America. Most of the family men had been coal miners in Wales. They brought their hard-work ethic to America, and it drove their children all their lives.

My grandpa had dark-olive skin and was a strong, barrel-chested man. He never worked out. His "workout" was his work. As part of his job at the flour mill, he often had to carry 100-pound sacks of flour. Relatives say he could grab two at a time, one in each hand, and flip them both up onto his broad shoulders.

Grandpa was also a man of few words. So when he did talk, I listened. I deeply respected my grandpa . . . and kind of feared him, too. He was one guy I didn't want to make mad.

While Grandpa was strong, he was no street fighter. Many of his children got caught up in the street fighting of the neighborhood, but he tried to avoid it. He was too busy working to put food on the table.

And he was a churchgoing man. For decades Grandpa and Grandma went to Bethany Baptist Church in north Denver. They took their children every Sunday. But as the kids matured into the teen years, most of them were more interested in street fighting than church. But through it all Grandma and Grandpa went to Bethany Baptist. And from the time I can remember, they took me with them. That's where I learned the basic Bible stories. That's where I trusted in Jesus.

Because Grandpa was so strong and about the only adult male figure consistently in my life, he became my father figure throughout my early years. I longed to hear the words "good job" from him whenever I did something well.

Twice a year I would look forward to report-card day. From the time I started going to Arvada Christian School I began to study really hard. My goal was to get straight A's. Why? Because when I was in seventh grade, Grandpa started a tradition. He would give me a dollar for every A that I received on my semester report card.

From the time I was in seventh grade through my senior year I got straight A's and ended up graduating with a 4.0. Why? Was it because I was so smart? No. As a matter of fact I'm kind of a slow learner, so what I lacked in learning ability I had to make up for in hard work.

No, the reason I got A's was because of Grandpa. I knew what would happen when I handed him my report card. He'd put on his reading glasses, open up the envelope, and look down the columns for the letter that he was hoping to see. He would then reach for his wallet, open it up, and give me one dollar for every A earned.

But then he would do something that would propel me forward for another semester of hard work. He would say, "Good job, Greg."

It wasn't the money that motivated me. I just wanted the main father figure in my life to be proud of me. When I knew that Grandpa was proud of me, I felt like I could conquer the world!

In some ways I'm still working for those words. But not from Grandpa, but from Jesus.

You see, we will stand before Him one day with our life report cards. He will scan the columns of our lives to see how we did. He will reach into His wallet (so to speak) and reward us for every A. But ultimately, what we all long to hear is "Good job."

The Big Q: Is there a judgment day, and what difference should it make in my life?

Here's how the Bible puts it in 2 Corinthians 5:10: "For we must all appear before the judgment seat of Christ, that each one may receive what is due him for the things done while in the body, whether good or bad."

The words *judgment seat* here mean "reward platform." Think how proud Olympic athletes are when they receive an Olympic medal as a result of their many years of hard work, discipline, and skill. But the heavenly reward platform is for eternal rewards, not earthly medals. This is where Jesus will sit, evaluate our lives as His children (both the good and the bad), and then reward us accordingly.

On this day He will evaluate our lives: "So then, each of us will give an account of himself to God" (Romans 14:12). He will evaluate our motives: "Therefore judge nothing before the appointed time; wait till the Lord comes. He will bring to light what is hidden in darkness and will expose the motives of men's hearts. At that time each will receive his praise from God" (1 Corinthians 4:5). He will evaluate our words: "But I tell you that men will have to give account on the day of judgment for every careless word they have spoken" (Matthew 12:36).

How did the apostle Paul feel about this judgment day? He had mixed emotions. On one side he was terrified by it. Right after mentioning the judgment day in 2 Corinthians 5:10, he shared his emotions in verse 11: "Since, then, we know what it is to fear the Lord, we try to persuade men."

Paul was petrified at the thought of standing before Jesus and having his life evaluated top to bottom, inside and out. Now if the great apostle Paul, who single-handedly reached much of the ancient world with the gospel of Jesus Christ, was terrified at the thought of judgment day, we may want to be afraid as well.

This fear, though, is not fear of being accused by Jesus, but fear of not hearing "Good job" or more appropriately, not hearing "Well done My good and faithful servant." It's fear of not having Him place rewards on our heads and rewards in our hands.

 INSANE BRAIN STRAIN
If one day we will have to give an account for every aspect of our lives before God Himself, why do we continue to disobey Him?

Now you may be thinking, *Well, I'm not motivated by that stuff.* Well, you should be. Why? Because Jesus wants you to be! As a matter of fact, He commands you to be! Check out Matthew 6:19-21:

> "Do not store up for yourselves treasures on earth, where moth and rust destroy, and where thieves break in and steal. But store up for yourselves treasures in heaven, where moth and rust do not destroy, and where thieves do not break in and steal. For where your treasure is, there your heart will be also."

The Bible talks about gold, silver, precious stones, and crowns. And if that weren't enough, Scripture even talks about cities that we will rule over. The amount of reward and responsibility depends on how faithfully we served Him on this side of eternity. Their value is not in what they are, but what they represent—the smile of Jesus! They are a constant reminder of His words "Well done." We will carry these treasures, these reminders of a life well lived for Christ, throughout eternity!

But what about those of us who don't get heavenly bling on that day? What happens to us? Because the judgment seat of Christ is only for Christians, and because all believers have as their foundation Jesus Christ, even the ones who fail to serve Him will still live with Him eternally. Look at the description of the guy whose worthless works burn up completely before the presence of Jesus: "He will suffer loss; he himself will be saved, but only as one escaping through the flames" (1 Corinthians 3:15).

So which one will you be? Will you be one who receives a ton of rewards and hears "Well done" from the Son of God . . . or will you be in heaven, saved by grace, but with your clothes smelling like smoke because you barely made it through the flames of judgment?

The apostle Paul had feelings of fear about judgment day, but he also was excited by it. Listen to his words in 2 Timothy 4:8: "Now there is in store for me the crown of righteousness, which the Lord, the righteous Judge, will award to me on that day—and not only to me, but also to all who have longed for his appearing." In many ways, Paul was motivated by a longing for and fear of the judgment seat of Christ.

We should be too.

And what about the judgment day for those who are not true Christians? It's a whole different day with a whole different outcome. Check out Revelation 20:11–15 for more on that sad subject.

Go Figure!

Now read Revelation 20:11-15 and answer these questions:

1. Will anyone escape this judgment day? Why or why not?

_____

_____

_____

2. What happens to a person whose name is missing from the Book of Life?

_____

_____

_____

3. Will judgment day come as a surprise to anyone? Why or why not?

_____

_____

_____

Read Hebrews 9:27-28. Answer these questions:

4. If everyone is destined to die once, what does that say about reincarnation?

_____

_____

_____

5. How does it make you feel knowing that one day you will be judged?

_____

_____

_____

6. Would you say that you are a Christian who is "waiting" for Christ? Why or why not?

_____

_____

_____

So What?

If life was set up in a way that there was no judgment day or after-life, then what you did, said, and thought on a daily basis really wouldn't matter in the long run. But life is not set up that way. There is a judgment day, and you don't have a choice in showing up for it. This truth should be permanently etched in your brain and permanently woven into the fabric of your life. What you do matters, both now and on that daunting day in the future. This truth should also motivate you to warn people who don't know Christ about what will happen if they don't put their trust in Him for salvation.

I can't help but think of Grandpa with his reading glasses and his open wallet when I think of judgment day. I long to hear the words "Well done, son" from my real Father figure, God.

How about you?

YOU'RE NEXT!

First Corinthians 3:11-15 uses the imagery of gold, silver, and costly stones to describe the things we've done in life that will survive the test of fire on judgment day. Wood, hay, and straw are used to describe those things of no eternal value—things that burn up on judgment day. Think back on all the time that has passed since you trusted Christ. There are two columns provided below. Underneath the Gold, Silver, Costly Stones column, jot down some of the things you've done for God that you think will make it through the fire that "will test the quality" of your work on earth. Here are a few examples:

The time I shared my faith with a friend.

The time I helped out at a rescue mission.

The time I spent worshiping God.

Underneath the Wood, Hay, Straw column, jot down some of the things you think will burn up on judgment day. Here are a few examples:

The time I wasted on the Internet.

The time I ignored a friend in need.

The time I prayed in public, but my motive was to look "spiritual."

Gold, Silver, Costly Stones	Wood, Hay, Straw
_____	_____
_____	_____
_____	_____
_____	_____
_____	_____
_____	_____

✳ ✳ ✳

For more info on **The Big Q: Is there a judgment day, and what difference should it make in my life?** visit www.dare2share.org/ soul fuel/archives and check out *Soul Fuel* question #17.

CHAPTER 17

The Cloud that Haunts Me Still

I used to stare at the big, billowy cumulonimbus clouds that would swirl by the window of my little Christian school classroom. Why? Because I was bored? No! Because my teachers used to tell me Jesus was coming back one day on one of them, and I needed to be ready. I would think about Jesus coming back. My teachers would point to verses like 1 Thessalonians 4:16-17:

> For the Lord himself will come down from heaven, with a loud command, with the voice of the archangel and with the trumpet call of God, and the dead in Christ will rise first. After that, we who are still alive and are left will be caught up together with them in the clouds to meet the Lord in the air. And so we will be with the Lord forever.

Back when I was about thirteenish, Yankee showed this really cheesy Christian movie called *A Thief in the Night*. But in spite of the horrific handlebar mustaches, the psychedelic polyester clothes, and the, shall we say, less than stellar performances, the movie worked for me. The whole idea of Jesus coming back and some people not being ready really freaked me out.

I remember walking out of our church on a Sunday night after having seen this movie, ready to reach the world by myself. The Antichrist, the mark of the beast, the return of Jesus, and all that crazy end-time stuff had done its job—it had turned me into a lean, mean witnessing machine.

There was a song in the movie called "I Wish We'd All Been Ready" by Larry Norman. The last lines, "The Father spoke, / the demons dined, / the Son has come and you've been left behind," stuck in my adolescent brain.

I didn't even really know what that meant at the time (and I'm still not sure I do), but all I knew was that it sounded pretty scary. I didn't want to be left behind, left out, or left wanting.

That primal fear motivated me to get busy when it came to serving Jesus with all my heart. The prospect of His showing up unannounced excited me, but it also intimidated me. Was I ready for His return? Was I living the kind of life that would make Him proud?

BLAST FROM THE PAST

To me, the second coming is the perpetual light in the path which makes the present bearable. I never lay my head on my pillow without thinking that maybe before the morning breaks the final morning may have dawned. I never begin my work without thinking perhaps he may interrupt my work and begin his own.[1]

—G. CAMPBELL MORGAN, 20TH CENTURY PREACHER

And regardless of where you stand when it comes to the return of Jesus—such as is He coming back before, during, or after the tribulation? Is there a literal rapture at all? Is there a literal seven-year tribulation? A literal 1,000-year period of time called the Millennium?—you have to agree to one insurmountable truth in the Bible: Jesus is coming back, and we need to be ready.

Often we as believers squabble over questions that sometimes miss the bigger picture. Regardless of your view of the end times, all of us should agree that a big part of our motivation to serve Jesus now is that He could come back at any time and that we need to be ready for His return.

The Big Q: How should the return of Christ impact my life?

We see this call to readiness all over the Bible, especially the Gospels. Check out these words of Jesus in Matthew 24:36-44:

> No one knows about that day or hour, not even the angels in heaven, nor the Son, but only the Father. As it was in the days of Noah, so it will be at the coming of the Son of Man. For in the days before the flood, people were eating and drinking, marrying and giving in marriage, up to the day Noah entered the ark; and they knew nothing about what would happen until the flood came and took them all away. That is how it will be at the coming of the Son of Man. Two men will be in the field; one will be taken and the other left. Two women will be grinding with a hand mill; one will be taken and the other left.
>
> Therefore keep watch, because you do not know on what day your Lord will come. But understand this: If the owner of the house had known at what time of night the thief was coming, he would have kept watch and would not have let his house be broken into. So you also must be ready, because the Son of Man will come at an hour when you do not expect him.

The application that I draw from this (regardless of my beliefs about the end times) is that Jesus is coming and I need to be ready. What does this readiness look like? Second Peter 3:10-15 tells us:

But the day of the Lord will come like a thief. The heavens will disappear with a roar; the elements will be destroyed by fire, and the earth and everything in it will be laid bare.

Since everything will be destroyed in this way, what kind of people ought you to be? You ought to live holy and godly lives as you look forward to the day of God and speed its coming. That day will bring about the destruction of the heavens by fire, and the elements will melt in the heat. But in keeping with his promise we are looking forward to a new heaven and a new earth, the home of righteousness.

So then, dear friends, since you are looking forward to this, make every effort to be found spotless, blameless and at peace with him. Bear in mind that our Lord's patience means salvation, just as our dear brother Paul also wrote you with the wisdom that God gave him.

 ## INSANE BRAIN STRAIN

If the main point of prophecy is that Jesus is coming back, then why do so many Christians miss the point when talking about the details of the of Jesus' return?

It tells us we should be ready by living godly lives, knowing that everything on this planet one day will be destroyed. This passage also strongly suggests that we should be ready by sharing our faith when it reminds us that "our Lord's patience means salvation. . . ." In other words, the longer Jesus takes to return, the more people will trust Christ, but only if we share the gospel with them!

So are you readying yourself by living a holy, "spotless" life? Are you ready because you have told everyone in your circle of influence the good news about Jesus?

Any prophecy about the end times, whether it is dealing directly with us or not, carries a reminder to everybody to get ready! Check out the last two verses of the Bible:

He who testifies to these things says, "Yes, I am coming soon." Amen. Come, Lord Jesus.

The grace of the Lord Jesus be with God's people. Amen. (Revelation 22:20-21)

Go Figure!

Open your Bible and read 1 Thessalonians 4:16-18. Answer these questions:

1. When Christ comes back, do you think most people will take notice? Why or why not?

   _____

   _____

   _____

2. Why does Christ need to come back a second time?

   _____

   _____

   _____

3. Why do you think God raises the dead first?

   _____

   _____

   _____

4. How does knowing this event could happen at any time make you feel?

_____

_____

_____

5. Does knowing about this event motivate you to share your faith with more urgency? Why or why not?

_____

_____

_____

6. How could you use this passage to "encourage each other"?

_____

_____

_____

The last two verses of the Bible are a powerful reminder that Jesus is coming soon. He could arrive any time, and we need to be ready! That is the big point of prophecy!

So What?

This truth should transform not only the way you look at clouds, but also the way you look at life! Think for a minute about how differently you would live if you knew Christ was coming back tomorrow. Guess what? He just might! The Bible is clear that one of the guiding attitudes of a Christian should be the hopeful expectation of Jesus returning at any minute. As the great preacher Theodore Epp said,

"Live as though Christ died yesterday, rose from the grave today, and is coming back tomorrow."[2]

So look to the clouds. Every day when you are outside, take a look straight up into the sky and focus on one big, billowy cloud. Could it be that one? Could that be the cloud that Jesus is returning on?

YOU'RE NEXT!

Take some time and write out a "Return of Christ Ready List," consisting of things you would take care of if you knew Jesus was coming back at 8 A.M. sharp tomorrow. (Use a separate piece of paper if you want to keep this private.) Here are a few examples to get you going:

I would share the gospel with these people: _____

I would get rid of the following things that I've been hiding: _____

I would apologize to my parents for _____

I would spend time in prayer, thanking God for _____

_____

_____

_____

_____

_____

_____

_____

✳ ✳ ✳

For more info on **The Big Q: How should the return of Christ impact my life?** visit www.dare2share.org/soulfuel/archives and check out *Soul Fuel* question #24.

CHAPTER 18

A Whole Lot of Shaking Going On

Mr. Ken Sanchez had an agenda with all the seventh- to tenth-grade boys who attended his "How to Interpret the Bible" class. We all knew what it was going into the class. The real purpose of this class was to raise up a small army of "preacher boys," potential competitors who could preach in the state and, perhaps someday, national preaching competitions for our Christian school association.

Now, there are certain words that should never be put together. Words such as the following:

Back Hair

Toe Mold

Stretch Marks

Skid Marks

Open Sore

Eye Pus

Embedded Tick

Tape Worm (Okay, I know it is one word, but . . .)

Semi Colon (See above)

Gravy Flavored (Thanks to my friend Rob Kelly for most of this list!)

Two more words that should never be used together are "preaching competition." The whole idea of a *preach-off* seems to kind of defeat the whole point of "the first shall be last and the last shall be first" thing.

Nevertheless, I was going to compete in this little contest. I worked hard to apply the questions: Who? What? When? Where? Why? and, last but not least, How? to my Bible passage of choice. I then identified what one thing the whole passage was saying, drew up a basic outline, pasted in transitions, added illustrations, and finally worked on an introduction and concluding illustration.

The problem was that when I went to stand behind the pulpit I was such a small 12-year-old that I could barely see above the pulpit. The three judges sat in the back, scribbling out their evaluations as I preached away.

Both my cold, sweaty hands grasped the sides of the pulpit as I preached. I was so scared I was literally rocking the wooden pulpit. The thing was actually rattling under my twitching, shaking grasp!

I'm sure the rattling sound of the pulpit got the judges' attention, and they looked up from their evaluation sheets and stared at me intently. The more I preached, the more I shook. The more I shook, the more they listened. By the time I was done, I was drenched in sweat (some things don't change!), and I went back to my seat and slouched way down in my chair, humiliated by my shaky performance.

When I got my evaluation back, not only had I passed, but I had won. I'll never forget reading the judges' evaluations. One of them wrote, "Great job! You were so intense you were literally shaking the pulpit!" What I knew was sheer fear, they mistook for intensity.

I was hooked. While I was never any good at team sports, I knew that preaching was going to be the "sport" I was going to attempt to excel in. From that day on, I knew that I was going to be a preacher or some kind of evangelist. I began to align my life toward that goal. This included getting books on preaching and poring over them. This meant going home, writing sermons, and practicing them in the mirror.

What was significant about the day I rattled the pulpit for the first time? It was the day that I discovered my spiritual gift of preaching. My mission in life started becoming clear that day.

The Big Q: What are spiritual gifts, and how do I discover mine?

A spiritual gift is a supernatural ability that God gives you at the moment you trust in Jesus as your Savior. Through His Holy Spirit who lives inside you, He gives you a gift, a gift that is meant to keep on giving, a supernatural ability to serve others in love.

Here is what the Bible says about spiritual gifts:

> There are different kinds of gifts, but the same Spirit. There are different kinds of service, but the same Lord. There are different kinds of working, but the same God works all of them in all men.
>
> Now to each one the manifestation of the Spirit is given for the common good. To one there is given through the Spirit the message of wisdom, to another the message of knowledge by means of the same Spirit, to another faith by the same Spirit, to another gifts of healing by that one Spirit, to another miraculous powers, to another prophecy, to another distinguishing between spirits, to another speaking in different kinds of tongues, and to still another the interpretation of tongues. All these are the work of one and the same Spirit, and he gives them to each one, just as he determines. (1 Corinthians 12:4-11)

There are all sorts of these spiritual gifts the Spirit of God gives to believers. But it's the same Spirit of God that unites us all.

So what is your spiritual gift?

Are you called to serve? To lead? To preach? To show mercy? To something else? There's only one way to find out, and that is by asking God to show you and then getting involved with different kinds of activities at your church or youth group (remember my chapter on the church?). Take a shot at teaching a Bible study, try some service projects, lead out in prayer, start a ministry, whatever.

The point is to keep trying different things until something kicks

> **BLAST FROM THE PAST**
>
> There is always the danger that we may just do the work for the sake of the work. This is where the respect and the love and the devotion come in—that we do it to God, to Christ, and that's why we try to do it as beautifully as possible.[1]
>
> —MOTHER TERESA, 20TH CENTURY FOUNDER OF THE MISSIONARIES OF CHARITY

in for you. Usually you will feel energized by your spiritual gift. You'll probably be pretty good at it and feel like it comes somewhat naturally to you. Once you discover your gifting, use that gift with maximum impact. Until you find your gift, keep trying different things.

 INSANE BRAIN STRAIN

What about the gifts of tongues and miracles? Are these gifts for today or were they more an early New Testament phenomenon? For further research read: 1 Corinthians 12–14.

One of the key passages of Scripture that deals with spiritual gifts is 1 Corinthians 13. Known as "the love chapter" by many, this passage is right between the two major chapters of the Bible that deal with spiritual gifts. Basically what this is telling us is that no matter what your spiritual gifting, the main thing is that you apply it in love. You could be the best preacher or encourager or prayer warrior in the world, but if you aren't exercising your spiritual gift in love, it's all a waste of time and effort.

Go Figure!

Read 1 Corinthians 13 and answer these questions:

1. How does God describe those who use their spiritual gift without love?

    _____

    _____

    _____

2. List the characteristics of love.

    _____

    _____

    _____

3. What will never fail? What will fade and what will not?

    _____

    _____

    _____

4. What is the greatest trait we can have?

    _____

    _____

    _____

5. On a scale from 1 to 10 (10 the highest) how much have you operated in love today?

_____

_____

_____

6. How can you remind yourself every day to love everyone you encounter?

_____

_____

_____

My wife has the gifts of mercy and encouragement. She loves people. What does she do for a living? She is a fifth-grade public school teacher. Why? So she can show mercy and encouragement to elementary school kids. She is excellent at it. Her spiritual gifts are demonstrated at our church, with her friends, and at her job. Her gifts have helped her find her calling.

So What?

Now that you know there is at least one powerful and needed spiritual gift inside you waiting to be unleashed, what are you waiting for? Get together with your youth leader and start a dialogue about what your gifting might be. I guarantee that there are definite places you could plug in—and I also guarantee you'll find incredible joy in fulfilling your God-given purpose!

I am a preacher. Why? Because when I was 12 years old, I nervously stood behind an old wooden pulpit and found my gifting and my calling.

It's your turn now.

YOU'RE NEXT!

Oftentimes our spiritual gifts line up with things we like to do naturally. Take some time to make a list of things that you are passionate about, then compare the list with the list of spiritual gifts in Romans 12. Here are some examples to get you started:

When I see someone who is hurting, I am passionate about listening to his or her problems and trying to help, so I probably have the gift of encouragement.

When I step into a situation that seems disorganized and purposeless, I am passionate about stepping up and getting things organized and on track, so I probably have the gift of leadership.

_____

_____

_____

_____

_____

_____

_____

_____

_____

_____

_____

✳ ✳ ✳

For more info on **The Big Q: What are spiritual gifts, and how do I discover mine?** visit www.dare2share.org/soulfuel/archives and check out *Soul Fuel* question #23.

CHAPTER 19

The Phone Call from Hell

O kay, prepare yourself. This is the weirdest thing I have ever experienced. I don't usually share this with teenagers—but it's too strange not to tell.

Now you've got to understand, while I'm a pretty intense guy, I don't buy a lot of the stuff out there that TV preachers say about their demonic encounters. Usually when I hear some sensational story about how some evangelist faced down the forces of darkness in some extravagant power encounter, one word usually comes to mind: Cuckoo!

I guess it's my turn to be mocked. But here goes . . .

It was the summer between my seventh- and eighth-grade years. I spent a lot of time with Spencer, my summer friend. We went to different schools during the school year, but over the hot school-free months we hung out and did all the stuff that normal 12-year-old boys do. We rode bikes, threw rocks, and all that jazz.

We also had another dynamic that made our friendship strong. God had given me the privilege of leading Spencer to Christ earlier that summer. I was training him in all the basic stuff about Christianity I had learned from my own studies, my church, and Arvada Christian School.

One day Spencer called me, and he was flat-out scared. He said that something strange was happening in his house. I asked him to tell me more. He didn't want to say much at first but finally asked, "Does the Bible say anything about ghosts?"

"Well, not a lot," I said, "but the Bible does talk about demons a lot, a whole lot. Why do you ask?"

Spencer explained that strange noises were coming from under his kitchen sink. Every time he opened up the little half-door under the sink, the noises would stop. It really freaked him that the noises sounded like voices.

I knew that ghosts were a myth but that demons were very real. "Well, Spencer," I said, "it sounds to me like you've got a demon problem." I probably sounded like some kind of supernatural-pest-control specialist.

He said with simple sincerity, "Greg, I'm scared. What do I do?"

I did the only thing my 12-year-old brain could think of at the time; I told him to put the phone under the kitchen sink, shut the door, and leave it there for a few minutes. I wanted to ask questions and see if the "thing" responded. I suggested Spencer go to another room to watch television or something for a few minutes.

I could hear the phone clunking around amidst cans of cleaning products and, of course, the forces of darkness. I had seen previews to the movie *The Exorcist* and so I asked the only question I'd seen there. To be honest, I felt like an idiot as I repeated, "What is your name? What is your name? What is your name?" I wasn't the brightest kid in the world, but you've got to give me an A for effort.

For the first few minutes I just sat there, feeling dumb and shaking my head, wondering what I had gotten myself into and what was taking so long. Suddenly I heard what sounded like a loud, throaty breath. Chills ran down my spine. Then I heard the creak of the door under the kitchen sink opening.

The next sound was Spencer's voice. He asked me if I had heard something. I said "Yes!" and begged him to put the phone back in and leave it there. Meanwhile I was scrambling for a tape recorder so I could record my encounter. This was no longer a joke. It felt dangerous. It was dangerous.

Armed with a fresh cassette tape in my recorder, I pressed Record and again started asking, "What is your name?" Just then the most demonic, scary, and hair-raising voice you can imagine screeched into the phone, "My name is no concern of yours."

I was so scared, I started shaking. This was not a human voice; no human I know of could manipulate that kind of sound into his vocal chords.

Not knowing any better, I started quoting verses and taunting this demonic presence. (By the way, that's a no-no. The Bible makes it clear in Jude 8 and 9 that we're never to talk smack to a demon like I did. But I was 12, so I think that God gave me grace in spite of my stupidity.) It responded angrily and began to go on about how the forces of evil were aligning and that they would overthrow Christ someday. This presence could manipulate the Bible and was trying to manipulate me.

My fear turned to anger. So I said something that I probably shouldn't have said. "Do you know what I'm going to do when I grow up just to make you mad?"

"What?" it said in its evil voice.

"I'm going to win this world to Jesus Christ."

That demon screamed so loudly that I had to put the phone away from me and pointed it at the tape recorder. By this time I was freaking out. Spencer had also heard the scream and he ripped open the door and grabbed the phone. "What happened?" he asked.

I told him to get out of the house and that I was coming over.

I grabbed my Bible and the tape recorder and ran down to

Spencer's house. I found him sitting on the porch, terrified. He was even more afraid when I played the tape recording for him.

Over the next hour or two we prayed, read Scripture, and asked God to remove the demon. As far as I know, nothing like that ever happened at Spencer's house again.

More than a decade later, I saw Spencer again while driving through the old neighborhood, and we talked about it. He swore up and down that whatever happened that day, he didn't make the noises on the other line. I believed him. I still do.

Now you may be thinking, *Cuckoo!*, and that's your choice. Who knows? Maybe it was somebody else who was playing some kind of elaborate trick on both of us. But I honestly believe that it was a demon and that it was my first (and hopefully only) verbal encounter with a demonic presence.

> **BLAST FROM THE PAST**
>
> As the devil showed great skill in tempting men . . . equal skill ought to be shown in saving them. The devil studied the nature of each man, seized upon the traits of his soul, adjusted himself to them and insinuated himself gradually into his victim's confidence—suggesting splendors to the ambitious, gain to the covetous, delight to the sensuous, and a false appearance of piety to the pious— and a winner of souls ought to act in the same cautious and skillful way.[1]
>
> —IGNATIUS LOYOLA, 16TH CENTURY FOUNDER OF THE JESUITS

I think God allowed it to happen to me at an early age so I would believe in the reality of the supernatural, so I would soak myself even more in Scripture and in prayer.

The Big Q: How do I engage in spiritual warfare?

Not on the phone, I guarantee you.

And while I want you to know that the power of Jesus can defeat any demon, there are more subtle, pervasive, and sinister evil threats to your walk with God. The Bible makes it clear that there is a war raging all around us. It's a battle between the forces of darkness and the kingdom of light for the souls of the lost. It's this battle you need to prepare for. Paul makes this clear in 2 Timothy 2:24-26:

> And the Lord's servant must not quarrel; instead, he must be kind to everyone, able to teach, not resentful. Those who oppose him he must gently instruct, in the hope that God will grant them repentance leading them to a knowledge of the truth, and that they will come to their senses and escape from the trap of the devil, who has taken them captive to do his will.

Our goal is to set captives free. But Satan will not easily give up his prisoners. Hence, the bloody struggle.

 ## INSANE BRAIN STRAIN

Why does God allow spiritual warfare to go on at all, when He could just protect us from the enemy at all times?

But it's not just a battle for their souls; it's also a battle for our hearts and minds. The devil and his cohorts want to deceive, distract, and destroy us. Whether it be through sexual temptation, pride, or selfishness, they will do their best to trip us up and beat us down.

So how do we fight back and win? The answer is tucked away in Ephesians 6:10-20:

> Finally, be strong in the Lord and in his mighty power. Put on the full armor of God so that you can take your stand against the

devil's schemes. For our struggle is not against flesh and blood, but against the rulers, against the authorities, against the powers of this dark world and against the spiritual forces of evil in the heavenly realms. Therefore put on the full armor of God, so that when the day of evil comes, you may be able to stand your ground, and after you have done everything, to stand. Stand firm then, with the belt of truth buckled around your waist, with the breastplate of righteousness in place, and with your feet fitted with the readiness that comes from the gospel of peace. In addition to all this, take up the shield of faith, with which you can extinguish all the flaming arrows of the evil one. Take the helmet of salvation and the sword of the Spirit, which is the word of God. And pray in the Spirit on all occasions with all kinds of prayers and requests. With this in mind, be alert and always keep on praying for all the saints.

Pray also for me, that whenever I open my mouth, words may be given me so that I will fearlessly make known the mystery of the gospel, for which I am an ambassador in chains. Pray that I may declare it fearlessly, as I should.

Go Figure!

Open your Bible and read 1 Peter 5:8-11. Ask for God's insight as you answer these questions:

1. In what ways does Satan "devour" people like a lion?

_____

_____

_____

2. What does it mean to be "self-controlled and alert"?

_____

_____

_____

3. What are some specific ways you could "resist" the devil?

_____

_____

_____

4. Does it help you to know that you're not alone in spiritual warfare? Why or why not?

_____

_____

_____

5. Why does God allow us to suffer for a little while?

_____

_____

_____

6. Would you consider yourself to be "strong, firm, and steadfast"? Why or why not?

_____

_____

_____

God has given you a protective suit of spiritual armor to wear in your battle against Satan. These pieces of armor represent the spiritual provision God has given each of us to protect us from Satan's relentless and ruthless attacks. Here is the gear He has for us:

His personal power: As we walk in a daily declaration of dependence on His Holy Spirit (more on that later) Satan can't touch us.

The belt of truth: This represents the life of consistency, honesty, and integrity that we are called to live out.

The breastplate of righteousness: These are the daily choices we make, in His power, to do what is right no matter what.

The boots of readiness: This is being ready, willing, and able to share the message of Jesus with everyone we encounter.

The shield of faith: This is when we choose to hide behind the truths of God's Word instead of buying the lies of Satan.

The helmet of salvation: This represents having confidence in the message of the gospel and knowing that we are a child of God.

The sword of the Spirit: These are the verses of Scripture that we use and quote (just as Jesus did against Satan in Matthew 4) in times of temptation are our defense.

Prayer: All of the armor that God provides and His personal reservoir of power are a prayer away. We ask God to control us, and we choose to submit and Satan runs . . . every time.

So What?

You probably don't have a demon lurking in the pipes below your kitchen sink, but you definitely have some lurking in your world. The fact is, a spiritual battle is going on all around you, and if you choose not to fight, you choose to lose. The key is to remember to live in the power of the Spirit, be constant in prayer, and put on your armor every day. I don't know about you, but ending up as lion chow doesn't sound very appealing to me!

In about four decades years on this planet I believe I've had one verbal encounter with a demon, but I have had countless other nonverbal ones that are much more scary . . . and I think you may have too.

Satan and his well-organized army of powerful fallen angels work every single day. They are probably swirling somewhere nearby you right now, watching, waiting for just the right time to attack with just the right temptation to get us to do wrong.

To me, that is much scarier than a phone call from hell.

YOU'RE NEXT!

Satan will try to attack you in specific areas of your life. Below is a list of the spiritual armor God has provided you. Go through each piece of armor and write down a specific area of your life for which you need the armor's protection.

For example, if every time you get on the Internet, Satan attacks you with the temptation to go to Web sites you know God wouldn't approve of. You need to put on the breastplate of righteousness in the power of the Spirit and pray for victory in this area.

You'd write: The breastplate of righteousness: When I use the Internet.

Or say you have a bad relationship with your dad, so sometimes the devil attacks you with thoughts that your heavenly Daddy doesn't love you or maybe has even abandoned you. You need to put on the helmet of salvation and remember that you are a child of God no matter what. You'd write: The helmet of salvation: Remember I am a child of God and loved by Him.

The armor of God

His personal power

_____

_____

The belt of truth

_____

_____

The breastplate of righteousness

_____

_____

The boots of readiness

_____

_____

The shield of faith

_____

_____

The helmet of salvation

_____

_____

The sword of the Spirit

_____

_____

Prayer

_____

_____

✳ ✳ ✳

For more info on **The Big Q: How do I engage in spiritual warfare?**
visit www.dare2share.org/soulfuel/archives and check out *Soul Fuel*
question #21.

CHAPTER 20

Salvation and Seizures

Doug is my big brother, and I love him. If you knew him, you would love him, too. He may be the most innocent soul I have encountered on this planet. He is sincere and straightforward. Think Rocky Balboa without the strong Philadelphia accent, throw in a whole lot of love for his fellow man, and you pretty much have my brother pegged.

In his younger years, back when we lived in the heart of the city, Doug struggled. Maybe it was because he seemed so childlike and innocent. Maybe it was because he smiled so much and always seemed to be whistling a tune with his lips and with his heart. Maybe it was because he seemed like an easy target.

His epilepsy didn't help the situation at all. Ma was always afraid he was going to get in some serious altercation with some mean neighborhood kids. A fight, she was sure, would induce the seizure that would kill him.

Once Doug entered junior high school, things escalated in a violent way. While Doug was innocent and sincere, he wasn't afraid to get into a fight if he had to—so more and more teens tested him. Once one of the tougher teens threw him over a ledge at Lake Junior

High School to the hard concrete floor about 15 feet below. Luckily, he got away with just a sprained ankle.

Things were about to go really bad for Doug. Between the fights in and out of school, his personal challenges, and the standard angst of adolescence, Doug was in a battle. His innocence, for a time, was replaced with confusion. His sincerity was replaced with anger.

Then it wasn't just inside of school that Doug was starting to struggle; it was outside of school as well. He began having brushes with the law, never for anything major, but they could have easily started spiraling out of control.

When we moved to the 'burbs and started going to Youth Ranch and Yankee's church, I started seeing changes in my big brother. What sealed the deal was when he went off to a Christian camp in Florida for a week. He came back a changed teen.

I could go on and on about story after story of Doug sharing his faith with neighbors, friends, strangers, anybody and everybody who would listen. Doug didn't necessarily know exactly how to bring it up smoothly. He just brought it up. And the strange thing is that, for the most part, people listened.

When he finally could afford a car, he took that car, as he had his bike before then, all over Denver, doing drive-by evangelism. He didn't know any better.

Praise God.

One time he pulled up to a stop sign in his car and noticed that a guy pulled up behind him. He thought, *That guy needs Jesus.* He slammed his car in park and got out. The poor guy probably thought that this teenager was mad about something and wanted to fight. Instead, Doug started sharing the gospel with the stunned man.

Other cars, gathering behind in a line, started to honk with impatience. Doug looked back, smiled, raised up his hand in a welcoming wave, and said, "Hold on! I'll be to you in a minute!"

After Doug got out of high school, he met a waitress at a local restaurant whom he thought was really cute. Because he had a standard of dating only Christians, he led her to Christ and then asked her out. She said yes. On their second date he asked her to marry him. She thought he was kidding, so she said yes.

He wasn't kidding.

Six months later they got married. They've been married ever since. And Doug is still faithfully sharing the gospel with anybody and everybody who will listen.

People ask me why I'm so intense for the gospel, why I'm more than willing to work the long hours and travel across the United States, training teens through Dare 2 Share conferences to know and share their faith in Jesus. My answer is simple: Doug Stier.

He's my big brother. He's my hero. As a preteen, I watched my 18-year-old brother surrender himself completely to the fulfillment of the Great Commission. He didn't let the fact that he had epilepsy or his background or disabilities get in the way. Doug simply shared Jesus with a sweet smile and innocent heart. Why do I take the Great Commission so seriously? Because I saw it lived out in him.

> **BLAST FROM THE PAST**
>
> Some people love to dwell near church with choir and steeple bell. But I want to run a rescue station a yard from the gates of hell.[1]
>
> —C. T. Studd, 19th century missionary to China, India, and Africa

The Big Q: What is the Great Commission, and how does it relate to me?

It is the final and lasting commandment of Jesus to His disciples and to us. After He died and rose again He appeared to His disciples several times. On one of these occasions He commissioned them to change the world in His name and with His gospel.

> Then Jesus came to them and said, "All authority in heaven and on earth has been given to me. Therefore go and make disciples of all nations, baptizing them in the name of the Father and of the Son and of the Holy Spirit, and teaching them to obey everything I have commanded you. And surely I am with you always, to the very end of the age." (Matthew 28:18-20)

Jesus is giving us one command that breaks into three parts:

1. You have the right to share the truth!

Jesus is reminding us that He is fully authorizing us to share the truth of the gospel with the entire planet! Jesus is the supreme ruler of the universe, and as the Lord of all, He is authorizing you to share the gospel with anyone and everyone.

Especially in today's culture of extreme tolerance, where Jesus claiming to be the only way to heaven (John 14:6) is NOT cool, you have to heed the words of Jesus. He has given you the right to share Jesus. Even if your friends say you shouldn't. Even if someday the law says you shouldn't. Even if you take heat for it at school.

You have been authorized by the most powerful being in the universe to declare the message of truth to everyone; Share it in love!

 ## INSANE BRAIN STRAIN

According to the Bible, the Great Commission is not optional, and neither is obeying the law. What if one day we pass a law that makes it illegal to obey the Great Commission?

2. You have the responsibility to share the truth!

Jesus tells us to "go and make disciples. . . ." Does this sound optional to you? This includes sharing the gospel message and then training those who accept it to put into practice what they have learned from the Bible.

Go Figure!

Open your Bible and read 1 Corinthians 9:16-17.

1. What does it mean to "preach the gospel"?

   _____

   _____

   _____

2. How else could you phrase "preach the gospel"?

   _____

   _____

   _____

3. Why did Paul feel "compelled" to preach the gospel? Are we also compelled?

   _____

   _____

   _____

4. Would Paul have felt bad if he didn't share his faith? Why do you say that?

   _____

   _____

   _____

5. What happens when we voluntarily help fulfill the Great Commission? And what is your first step?

_____

_____

_____

_____

The idea of "go" is literally "as you are going." In other words, as you go to school you should be making disciples, as you go to soccer practice, or to dance class, or on vacation, or whatever, you should be making disciples. We are to do it everywhere and all the time!

So are you? Are you seeking to reach a friend for Jesus right now?

But making disciples is more than just *going wide* with the gospel message. That's an essential part of it, but it is only half the equation. The second half is helping those you lead to Jesus *grow deep* in the truth. Jesus put it this way: "…teaching them to obey everything I have commanded you." What does this mean? It means helping them know the truth and then helping them put it into practice.

3. You have the reason to share the truth!

Jesus tells us in these verses that He is with us always. He will never leave us or forsake us. He is there to encourage us and stand by us as we seek to carry on the mission that the disciples got started.

Isn't that awesome? You are not alone in your quest.

Maybe that's why Doug is so happy all the time. He knows that as he goes and makes disciples in his world, he is not alone. Neither are you!

So What?

Jesus is with you as you go and share His message. The question is *Are you ready to do your part?* There are no two ways about it. If you are not doing your part to help fulfill the Great Commission, you are living in disobedience to God and missing out on the greatest mission on earth. If you truly believe that those who die without trusting in Christ spend eternity in hell, you really shouldn't have a problem being motivated to share your faith. Remember, Jesus' last command to us is called the Great Commission, not the Good Suggestion. And never ever forget that He is with you every step of the way!

YOU'RE NEXT!

Think of one person you know who doesn't know Jesus as his or her Savior and make a decision to tell that person the good news of Jesus within the next 48 hours. Why 48 hours? Because studies show that if you don't do what you learned in 48 hours, then the chances are that you will never do it at all. Why 48 hours? Because that friend could be dead and gone before you know it. Car wrecks and accidents claim a lot of lives, both young and old.

Maybe this means that you send that friend an e-mail, get into an online discussion, call him or her up on the phone, or meet him or her at your nearest Starbucks. Whatever it means for you, take the challenge and then log on to www.gregstier.org and tell me what happened. Will you take The 48 Hour Challenge. Check the box yes or no.

❏ YES   ❏ NO

✳ ✳ ✳

For more info on **The Big Q: What is the Great Commission and how does it relate to me?** visit www.dare2share.org/soulfuel/archives and check out *Soul Fuel* question #15.

Leading a group of fellow teenagers in a Bible study
before we headed out for Friday Night Soulwinning

CHAPTER 21

Me, Art, and Billy

O ne of my best teen friends was Art. He was a big, tall kid with a small head who had really light skin. I used to call him the "albino rhino."

When Art got obsessed with doing something, he did it with all of his heart. In high school he decided to take up weight lifting. Soon he was bench-pressing more than 300 pounds. When he decided to memorize the book of Romans—that's more than 400 verses—he did it in three weeks.

Suffice it to say that when Art set his mind to doing something, he did it. And so did I. We were both kind of obsessed teenagers who went full tilt toward every goal we set. This was especially true when it came to sharing the gospel.

Every summer Art and I would spend countless hours at the Westminster Mall, sharing the gospel with other teenagers. We would go into the bookstore and put gospel pamphlets called tracts into all the occult books (not recommended). In the department stores we would put tracts into the mannequins' outstretched hands (not recommended). We would even take tracts, unroll the toilet paper in the guys' bathrooms, stick a tract in there, and roll the toilet paper back up (highly recommended!). Why? Because we knew that when people were just sitting there they wanted something to read!

And because we were on a quest to reach the world for Jesus all by ourselves if we had to!

In addition, my church asked me to lead an outreach ministry called Friday Night Soulwinning. Yankee and his crew never underestimated teenagers; they truly believed we could do the jobs given to us.

Every Friday night I would gather as many teenagers as I could, break them into groups, and send them out to the major shopping malls. Once there, they would share the gospel with as many teenagers as possible. After a few hours we would gather back and share stories, collect follow-up cards, and pray.

My goal was to get all the people on the planet to trust in Jesus as their Savior! All totaled throughout my junior high and high school years I estimate that I personally witnessed to at least 5,000 others. But I knew that 5,000 was a drop in the bucket compared to the five billion people who were on the planet. So I recruited Art. Together we made a powerful dynamic duo of evangelism. But it wasn't enough. So I started leading Friday Night Soulwinning. But that wasn't enough either.

Then one night when I was watching television, I saw an interview with the great evangelist Billy Graham who had reached millions with the gospel. Watching this interview surprised me and changed me forever. The reporter asked Billy Graham a question about his ministry's impact on the world. Graham responded that they really hadn't even begun to make a dent.

That hit me hard. I'll never forget thinking that if Billy Graham and his worldwide ministry hadn't even made a dent, then surely I couldn't. I began to realize that it would take more than me and Art and the teens from Friday Night Soulwinning. It would take an entire army.

That's when the whole idea of multiplication invaded my mind. I calculated that if we could train other youth groups in the area to share their faith effectively, then we would multiply our efforts. And so, as a teenager, I began to equip other teenagers to share the gospel. All of this eventually led to the vision for starting Dare 2 Share. Our mission from day one has been to multiply the impact of the gospel by training teenagers to transform their world. My lifelong dream of raising up an army of teen "proclaimers" comes true every day. But to be honest, like my hero Billy Graham, we haven't even begun to make a dent.

Now we are speeding past seven billion people on the planet, a large percentage of whom have never heard and will likely never hear the gospel message. What happens to them when they die? This disturbing question racked my hyperactive teenage brain.

The Big Q: What about people who have never heard the gospel?

There is no need for an Insane Brain Strain in this chapter. The Big Q is just that. Out of all the questions that people ask me about God, sin, life, and death, this is probably the toughest one.

The problem is that the Bible makes it crystal clear that there is only one way into heaven. Acts 4:12 leaves no wiggle room on this point: "Salvation is found in no one else, for there is no other name under heaven given to men by which we must be saved."

The "name under heaven" the apostles are talking about here is Jesus Christ. John put it this way in John 3:36: "Whoever believes in the Son has eternal life, but whoever rejects the Son will not see life, for God's wrath remains on him."

Listen to the words of Jesus in John 3:17-18: "For God did not send his Son into the world to condemn the world, but to save the world through him. Whoever believes in him is not condemned, but whoever does not believe stands condemned already because he has not believed in the name of God's one and only Son."

Jesus is the only way to heaven—and those who don't believe in Him spend an eternity in hell. That's the raw reality behind these sobering passages and the others like them throughout the New Testament.

Is that fair?

In one sense, the only truly fair thing would be if God sent everybody to hell. We all sin and fall short of God's perfect standard. The consequences of that sin is death. So if God condemned everybody to hell, He would be perfectly justified in doing so.

But God is merciful. That's why He sacrificed His only Son, to make the way for us to be adopted into His family. He allowed His Son to be mocked, mutilated, and murdered so that we could spend an eternity with Him.

If you think about it, God has left everyone on this planet some pretty powerful indicators of His presence. For one, He created this awesomely beautiful planet to show us that there is Something, Someone bigger than we are who designed it all. You can tell from the warmth of the sun that God is a kind God. You can tell from the power of a thunderstorm that God is a strong God. Psalm 19:1-4 contains a powerful string of verses that show how much you can tell about God from just looking around at the universe.

> The heavens declare the glory of God;
> the skies proclaim the work of his hands.
> Day after day they pour forth speech;
> night after night they display knowledge.
> There is no speech or language
> where their voice is not heard.

Their voice goes out into all the earth,
their words to the ends of the world.

In this passage all of nature is described as a megaphone, a loud-speaker, that continuously calls out to every human everywhere that there is a God. That's the first step toward finding Jesus: believing God exists and wants to care for us and communicate with us.

If people follow the bread-crumb trail that all of creation has left for them, at the end of the trail, they will find the gospel message. In other words, I believe that if people are open to it, God will find a way for them to hear the gospel message. Maybe this is the same thing that the apostle Paul was getting at in Acts 17:26-27: "From one man he made every nation of men, that they should inhabit the whole earth; and he determined the times set for them and the exact places where they should live. God did this so that men would seek him and perhaps reach out for him and find him, though he is not far from each one of us."

God isn't far from anybody. His power demonstrates to all men everywhere that He exists and is waiting for them to respond to the clues and cues evident in the breathtaking nature all around us.

Not only does nature testify to the existence of one God who cre-ated everything, there is another testimony that is inside each of us. Down deep inside the soul of every human, there is something that relentlessly and loudly points to the true God. Romans 1 puts it this way:

For since the creation of the world God's invisible qualities—his eter-nal power and divine nature—have been clearly seen, being under-stood from what has been made, so that men are without excuse.

For although they knew God, they neither glorified him as

God nor gave thanks to him, but their thinking became futile and their foolish hearts were darkened. Although they claimed to be wise, they became fools and exchanged the glory of the immortal God for images made to look like mortal man and birds and animals and reptiles. (vv. 20-23)

If you just glanced over these verses, read them again . . . slowly. Drink in what this passage of the Bible is saying. Down deep inside, everybody knows that there is one true God, but they avoid this God like a selfish child who puts a finger in each ear and sings a song so that he doesn't have to hear his dad's voice calling him.

God is making it crystal clear that somewhere in the secret chambers of each human heart, everyone knows there is a God whom they must give an account to someday. But instead of responding to Him, they "suppress the truth by their wickedness" (v. 18) and "exchange the glory of the immortal God" for a lie.

What's the result of all this denial? Sinful humanity stands before God without an excuse. Why? Because down deep inside everybody knows of the true God, and they run from Him and invent lesser, more compliant gods to take His place.

Go Figure!

Open your Bible and read Romans 10:13-15. Answer these questions:

1. According to this passage, will God turn away anyone who calls on Him?

_____

_____

_____

2. How would you answer each of the questions Paul is asking?

_____

_____

_____

3. What does God use to help get the gospel message to those who haven't heard?

_____

_____

_____

4. Do you feel like God is "sending" you to preach the gospel? Why or why not?

_____

_____

_____

5. In what ways are we all called to be missionaries?

_____

_____

_____

So What?

What does this have to do with you? Two main things: First of all, know that God is merciful and has left everyone with the flashing neon road signs of creation that point to His existence. If people respond to these clues and seek Him with all their hearts, He will find them.

Second, and most important for us, we are the ones called to do all we can to take the good news of Jesus to all people everywhere. Romans 10:13-14 says, "'Everyone who calls on the name of the

Lord will be saved.' How, then, can they call on the one they have not believed in? And how can they believe in the one of whom they have not heard? And how can they hear without someone preaching to them?"

We need to reach everyone around us with the gospel and be willing to either go or send others to share the gospel with those outside the gospel's reach. How do we send others? We pray for missionaries and support them financially.

Billy Graham realized he couldn't make a dent when it came to reaching everybody on the planet with the gospel. If Art and I led a thousand people to Christ a day, we wouldn't make a dent. But if all of us work together to reach those we can and support missionaries to reach those beyond our reach, not only will we make a dent, but everyone everywhere will hear the good news of Jesus.

Let's get busy.

> **BLAST FROM THE PAST**
>
> He [our Lord] does not say that the lost will never be saved if we don't go—He simply says, "Go therefore and make disciples of all the nations. . . ." He says, "Go on the basis of the revealed truth of My sovereignty, teaching and preaching out of your living experience of Me."[1]
>
> —OSWALD CHAMBERS, 19TH AND 20TH CENTURY MINISTER

YOU'RE NEXT!

One reason Art and I were able to share the gospel often and with success was our familiarity with our testimony (the story of how we trusted Christ). Write out your testimony so you can be ready to share it with others. Here's an outline to get you started.

My life before I trusted Christ.

The factors leading up to trusting Christ—I was going to Sunday school, my life seemed empty, so I turned to God, a friend took me to youth group/camp.

How my life changed after trusting Christ—be authentic; life still has problems and struggles, but now I have a relationship with the One who can truly help.

_____

_____

_____

_____

_____

_____

_____

_____

✳ ✳ ✳

For more info on **The Big Q: What about people who have never heard the gospel?** visit www.dare2share.org/soulfuel/archives and check out *Soul Fuel* question #14.

CHAPTER 22

Mace in My Face

I loved my grandma and grandpa. They were a tough old couple from inner-city Denver who told stories from the "old days" that blew me away. Not only did I love spending time with them, but I loved spending time at their house. Why? Because like most old people, they had a lot of interesting things stuffed away in old paint cans, back rooms, and dresser drawers.

One particular night when I was in junior high school, I decided to go downstairs in their basement and have fun digging through the stuff while they watched television. NOTE: This is a bad idea, not just because of the naughtiness of it but for (as you are about to see) the danger of it.

Opening up drawer after drawer of a huge dresser, I rummaged through the old-people stuff that filled each drawer to the top. There were 50-year-old pairs of grungy underwear (yuck!). Half-used tubes of Preparation H (yuck^2!). And lots and lots of buttons.

While I was musing about the buttons and wondering why the elderly are attracted to buttons like bees to pollen, something caught my attention in the corner of a drawer—a big, black can that had one giant word on it in large white letters: PARALYZER.

Now you probably understand that there are certain words that attract junior-high age boys, words like "explosion" and "ignite" and "danger." Well, you can add "PARALYZER" to the list. This boy was hooked.

As I picked up the can, it felt cool in my hands (in both senses of the word). I read the smaller print, and it went something like, "Danger! This is Mace. Do not spray in face."

Next I walked through a "thought" process that went something like, *Okay, this is Mace, but it's called "PARALYZER." Now, I've heard that Mace will mess you up. I've heard that it will make your eyes burn, but I've never heard that it would paralyze you in any way, shape, or form.* So I thought that I'd do a little experiment. I took the big, black can and shook it up as much as I could. I then sprayed it away from me, hoping that just a few molecules of the Mace would somehow make their way into my nasal passages so that I could disprove what I had come to dub "The Mace-Paralysis Theory." Anyway, nothing happened to me from the swirl of Mace molecules. So I thought that I'd spray again, but this time I would jump into the fog of Mace and breathe some of the molecules in.

Spray. Breathe. Nothing.

By this time I'm thinking, *Not only am I Mace-proof, I am Mace-retardant.*

Gaining more and more courage from my seeming immunity to this chemical concoction, I took a piece of paper, soaked it in Mace, put it up to my nose, and breathed in deeply.

Bad idea.

The Mace immediately ripped through my nasal cavity like an inferno of flames. My eyes became blinded by the salty liquid that was streaming like a river of fire from them. My face became absolutely numb, and it felt like I was losing feeling all over my body.

I began to scream hysterically, "It's true! I'm paralyzed! I'm paralyzed!"

I wasn't Mace-retardant. I was just retarded.

My grandmother shot up from her comfy chair and came running down the stairs (as fast as grandmothers can) screaming, "What's wrong? What's wrong?"

Because my lips and face were temporarily "paralyzed" by my liquid nemesis, I could barely get out the quasi-understandable words, "I'vveee sprayyyed Macccce in my faccce!"

She said, "What? I can't understand you, Greg."

I held up the black can of paint with the big white word "PARALYZER" pointed right at her. Next Grandpa came down, and he asked what happened. I tried to speak, but again to no avail. And besides, by this point my face was drenched with tears, snot, and saliva that had been pouring out of my facial orifices at a record and very gross rate. Grandpa simply said, "Boy, you've got problems," and returned upstairs to his show.

I knew he was right. I had some serious problems. These all started with my thinking people who invented, canned, and marketed Paralyzer had no clue what they were talking about. They did. As a result of my little basement experiment, I took labels and warnings seriously from that moment on . . . for the most part anyway. I began to believe the truth on the labels for my own good.

There are certain truths that we accept by faith. There are other ones that we learn from experience. But the bottom line is that there are truths.

The Big Q: What is truth, and can I know it with certainty?

Before Jesus was crucified, the Roman governor, Pilate, asked Jesus the question, "What is truth?" (John 18:38). This question is at the foundation of any belief system. How we interpret what truth is, and whether or not we can know it, impacts just about everything.

Although Jesus didn't answer Pilate's haunting question right then, He had already told His disciples, "I am the way and the truth and the life" (John 14:6). The ultimate answer to the question "What is truth?" is answered in the person of Jesus. Some say that truth should be defined as a "proposition or a principle." But true truth ultimately does not originate in a proposition or principle, but a person—Jesus Christ.

Real truth flows out of who Jesus is. Since He is the essence of truth, and since He created the universe, we see truth everywhere and in everything. The laws of physics and nature are truths. The basic principles of human interaction are based in the truths about how Jesus made us. And, of course, there are spiritual truths. As Christians, we look to the book of God (aka the Bible) to find the spiritual truths that we hold to in faith.

What is truth? Truth is what really is. It is reality, the actual facts, the way things really are. There is truth in science, history, math, and spirituality.

Yes, you may be thinking, *but I can test and see what is really true in science, history, and math. I can't really do that with spirituality.*

Not true.

 INSANE BRAIN STRAIN

If ultimate truth is found in God's Word, then why do so many run from it and try to define truth for themselves?

You can test the claims of any belief system and see if they are reality and based on actual facts or not. For instance, the Book of Mormon claims there was a lost tribe of Israel called the Nephites living in America thousands of years ago, yet there is not one shred of actual archaeological evidence to support it. That is something you can test. You can apply this same test to the Koran (the Muslim holy book), the Bhagavad Gita and Upanishads (the Hindu scriptures), and the Buddha's Four Noble Truths.

BLAST FROM THE PAST
The best evidence of our having the truth is our walking in the truth.[1]

—MATTHEW HENRY, 17TH AND 18TH CENTURY PASTOR AND BIBLE COMMENTATOR

And, yes, you can and should also test the Bible. As a matter of fact, God is not worried about the integrity of His truth. Check out what Jesus said about this in Luke 21:33: "Heaven and earth will pass away, but my words will never pass away."

The Word of God demonstrates again and again that it is truth (see chapter 10). It doesn't just claim it—it makes tons of totally outrageous predictions and then records how they were fulfilled exactly.

So in a way, we've defined truth as "the way things really are that ultimately flow from the God who really is." Science truth, math truth, all truths, flow from Jesus. And the book He gave us shows us the way things really are when it comes to spiritual realities. In other words, Jesus tells us the truth we should believe when it comes to the spiritual realm.

By this time you may feel that Mace has been sprayed, not in your face, but on your brain. You may feel that this stuff is way too intellectual for a 14-year-old, a 17-year-old, or a whatever-year-old to understand. Besides, it can't do any good in your life . . . right?

Wrong!

Remember that everything we do ultimately flows out of our view of truth. If we really believe the truth that our house is on fire, we will run out of it. If we really believe in the truth of the law of gravity, we will not go jump off a cliff. Our beliefs about what is really real determine everything that we do . . . everything!

Can we know truth? Yes! The book of Hebrews puts it this way: "Now faith is being sure of what we hope for and certain of what we do not see" (11:1). We Christians can know that God is God, the Bible is His Word, and Jesus is His Son. When it comes to Jesus, we can know that He died, rose, and is coming again. We can know that what He told us in His book is truth and that this truth can transform our lives. We can also know where we are going when we die (1 John 5:13) and how to live to the maximum before we die (John 10:10).

Okay, we can know truth. But can we know *all* truth? The answer is a big, fat NO! Why? Because we don't have the capacity! Only God knows all truth.

Go Figure!

Ask for God's help as you read Job chapters 40–42 and answer the following questions:

1. Why do you think God took Job on this tour of Animal Planet and the Nature Channel?

_____

_____

_____

2. How many questions did God ask Job during this tour?

_____

_____

_____

3. How many times did Job answer His questions?

_____

_____

4. What was Job's ultimate response to God's questions?

_____

_____

_____

5. What truth(s) did Job realize about God from all this?

_____

_____

_____

6. How does this apply to us in our quest for truth?

_____

_____

_____

The balance in all this is believing the clear truths of God's Word without being arrogant. There are some things we can know with certainty because God has made them clear. But there are a whole bunch of things that we can't be as confident about because the Bible isn't as clear about them.

So What?

Truth is what really is, and as a Christian you can know some truths with certainty. This certainty is the bedrock of your faith and will give you the confidence to share your faith in boldness to everyone God brings across your path.

So the next time you are at school and that one especially philosophical teacher goes off, claiming that nobody can know truth with certainty, raise your hand and ask him or her, "Is your claim true, and if it is, can you know it with certainty?" You will have just put a philosophical headlock on the teacher.

How does truth apply to you personally in your walk with God? Simple . . . believe His promises. When He tells you in Psalm 139:13-14 that you have been custom-made by God as a masterpiece, believe it! When He tells you in Philippians 4:13 that you can do everything through His strength, don't doubt it!

I pray that you will walk in humble confidence, that you will hold tightly and confidently to the clear truths of Scripture with one hand. With your other hand, may you seek to grasp the timeless truths of eternity that will cause you to worship the God who knows all truth and is the ultimate source of every truth in the universe.

What's the truth when it comes to a big, black can of Mace? Put it down, back away slowly, and go watch some television with your grandparents.

YOU'RE NEXT!

Write an imaginary three- to four-paragraph note to a friend who believes that all truth is relative, which means, "what's true for you is truth for *you*. What's true for me is truth for *me*. Your truth and my truth don't necessarily have to agree."

_____

_____

_____

_____

_____

_____

_____

_____

_____

_____

_____

_____

_____

_____

_____

_____

_____

_____

_____

* * *

For more info on **The Big Q: What is truth, and can I know it with certainty?** visit www.dare2share.org/soulfuel/archives and check out *Soul Fuel* question #9.

CHAPTER 23

Turnaround and Fadeaway

In seventh grade I started playing basketball for Arvada Christian School, but don't be impressed; it's not hard to make the team when there are only 10 guys trying to make the team. As a matter of fact, it was impossible *not* to make the team back then.

Now, I was and always will be athletically challenged. Somehow I missed the agility gene in our family pool. But what I lacked in talent I was determined to make up in hard work. So I practiced for hours.

Jump shots weren't my specialty. Neither were three-pointers or slam dunks. (It's difficult to do that when you can barely reach the net!) But out of all the shots that I loathed, the most dreaded was the layup. I knew that the vast majority of my layups would lead to a gigantic *CLANK!* sound as they reverberated off the bottom of the rim. Then the ball would inevitably bounce back toward my oversized, big-haired head.

The only shot that I had even a slim chance of making was a turnaround fadeaway jump shot. I owned that shot at least 30 percent of the time. Even when I missed that shot, it was okay because at least it looked good! After all, it was the splicing together of a turnaround move, a pushing back move, and a jump shot move. It was three moves in one. Not only was it a basketball shot, it was a shout to the Trinity by its very nature.

Let's just say that basketball wasn't my sport. But like I said, what I lacked in ability and agility, I tried to make up with hustle and muscle.

All to no avail.

But I did commandeer the bench during our basketball games like a wartime general. That eight-foot stretch of wood was my domain. If you dared to sit there you had better check in with me first. I was in charge of the towels and the water bottles until the coaches called me to take my unrightful place on the basketball court.

The coaches felt they could unleash me if the game was already decided. So if our team was up by 30 points or down by 30 points, it was show time for me. Then the crowd started to cheer, "Stier! Stier! Stier! Stier!"

When I was summoned to the court, complete with headband, writstbands, and, yes, knee pads, the crowd knew they were in for something special—a night of court comedy and sheer, unadulterated spastic effort. They knew that I would be diving for every loose ball, sprinting up and down the court the hardest I could every time. When I played defense, I would use my whole body to keep my opponents from making a shot, waving arms, twitching hands, churning legs and all. Suffice it to say that my court appearances, while not pretty, were quite entertaining.

Coach Adams used to hold me up as an example. In the sweaty locker room he used to say things like, "Look at Stier! The boy ain't got an ounce of athletic ability, but he is all over the court. If you guys had half the heart of Stier, we'd be champions!" This fueled my fire even more, and the inevitable result was more adrenaline-fueled play on the basketball court.

I'll never forget the time my Arvada Christian School Eagles were in a tournament with the dreaded Alexander Dawson Academy. This school was our nemesis, and we had to win this particular game to win the tournament. For some reason the coach put me in earlier than I expected. This was no blowout, and there were more than a few minutes left in the game. I thought, *Maybe this is my moment of glory!*

And then it happened. While playing my tenacious kind of arm-flailing, seizure-inducing defense, I somehow stole the ball. With lightning speed—if lightning takes 15 seconds to run 100 feet—I rumbled down the court. Time suspended as I made my way toward the basketball hoop. Everybody knew what was coming. Everyone knows that when you steal the ball and you are all by yourself you either slam it or do a layup. Which would it be? Well, let me put it this way: I surprised them all. That day, all by myself on the opposite side of the court, I stopped right under the basket and did a turnaround fadeaway jump shot . . . and missed.

Back to the bench for me, back where I belonged.

But to be honest, as bad as I was, it didn't bother me that I was a laughingstock on the hardwood. I just wanted to stay on the team. Why? Because of the impact that the basketball coaches had on my life.

Coach Adams and Coach Schweitzer especially encouraged me, challenged me, and helped mold me into a servant of the Lord Jesus. I could be happy for months because of one encouraging thing they said to me. When they challenged me on something in my game (whether it be on the court or in the game of life) I always took what they said seriously. They became father figures for me at a crucial time in my spiritual, emotional, and physical development.

There is someone in your world ready to be your coach in the spiritual realm. That Someone is the Holy Spirit. He is our divine "coach" who travels inside every believer to encourage, teach, train, convict, and transform. He is working hard to develop us into the ultimate player on the court of life. He's making us into something beyond Michael Jordan or Lebron James. He is pushing us to become like Jesus Christ.

The Big Q: Who is the Holy Spirit, and what does He do?

The Holy Spirit is the third Person of the Trinity (more on that later). He is God Himself, not some impersonal force or feeling. As the indwelling coach He is there to teach us and train us how to live a life that pleases God. As the author of the playbook (aka the Bible), He can teach us what it means as we read and study it. He can show us how to apply the truths within the pages of Scripture to our lives so that we can learn how to play to win.

 INSANE BRAIN STRAIN
How can the Holy Spirit live inside millions of people at the same time?

Let's take a quick look at the truth of who the Holy Spirit is, what He does, and the passages of the Bible that prove it.

Truth: The Holy Spirit is God.
"How is it that Satan has so filled your heart that you have lied to the Holy Spirit. . . ? You have not lied to men but to God." (Acts 5:3-4)

Truth: The Holy Spirit dwells inside every believer.

"And you also were included in Christ when you heard the word of truth, the gospel of your salvation. Having believed, you were marked in him with a seal, the promised Holy Spirit, who is a deposit guaranteeing our inheritance until the redemption of those who are God's possession—to the praise of his glory." (Ephesians 1:13-14)

"Do you not know that your body is a temple of the Holy Spirit, who is in you, whom you have received from God?" (1 Corinthians 6:19)

Truth: He gives us the power we need to serve God.

"I pray that out of his glorious riches he may strengthen you with power through his Spirit in your inner being." (Ephesians 3:16)

Truth: He teaches us the truth.

"The Counselor, the Holy Spirit, whom the Father will send in my name, will teach you all things and will remind you of everything I have said to you." (John 14:26)

Truth: He gives us supernatural gifts to serve others.

"All these are the work of one and the same Spirit, and he gives them to each one, just as he determines." (1 Corinthians 12:11)

Truth: He is transforming us to make us like Jesus.

"And we . . . are being transformed into his likeness with ever-increasing glory, which comes from the Lord, who is the Spirit." (2 Corinthians 3:18)

Truth: He convicts the world of sin.

"When he comes, he will convict the world of guilt in regard to sin." (John 16:8)

Truth: He saves lost souls.

"He saved us, not because of righteous things we had done, but because of his mercy. He saved us through the washing of rebirth and renewal by the Holy Spirit." (Titus 3:5)

The list of what the Holy Spirit does goes on and on and on. Suffice it to say that He is busy—very busy. His goal is to bring glory to Jesus, so that Jesus can bring glory to the Father. He does this by transforming our lives and the lives of those around us moment by moment, day after day.

Think of the Holy Spirit as a coach or a personal trainer. He wants to make you better, stronger, and faster. He wants you to be the best Christian that you can be so that your life brings maximum happiness to God.

BLAST FROM THE PAST

Come, Holy Ghost, for Thee I call,
Spirit of burning, come!
Refining fire, go through my heart,
illuminate my soul,
scatter Thy life through every part,
and sanctify the whole.[1]

—JOHN AND CHARLES WESLEY, 18TH CENTURY
FOUNDERS OF METHODISM

Go Figure!

Open your Bible and read Galatians 5:16-26.

1. What does it mean to "live by the Spirit"?

_____

_____

_____

_____

_____

2. What are some of the sinful desires of your sinful nature?

_____

_____

_____

_____

3. Have you ever felt the conflict between your sin nature and the Holy Spirit? Why or why not? If so, who wins more?

_____

_____

_____

_____

4. Which of the acts of the sinful nature from verses 19-21 describe you the most?

_____

_____

_____

_____

5. What is the serious warning Paul gives in verse 21?

_____

_____

_____

6. What is one way you can help make sure the Holy Spirit wins against your sin nature?

_____

_____

_____

So What?

Maybe your spiritual walk is like my turnaround fadeaway jump shot. Perhaps you have missed the basket completely and are living out an air ball in your service to God. Maybe it's the double dribble of a bad habit, or you have been "traveling" to the wrong Web sites, or maybe you have fouled somebody and aren't willing to fess up.

Whatever the violation, there is hope. The coach is living inside of you to encourage, restore, cleanse, train, and transform you to take it to the hoop. He won't give up until you dominate your game.

Game on!

YOU'RE NEXT!

The Bible teaches us that when we let the Holy Spirit fill us and control us, the character traits described in Galatians 5:22-23 flow out of our lives: "But the fruit of the Spirit is love, joy, peace, patience, kindness, goodness, faithfulness, gentleness and self-control."

Take some time and slowly read through the list below, then rate yourself on a scale of 1 to 10 on how evident each of the traits is in your life. Ask the Holy Spirit to help you improve on the areas with low ratings.

love	1 2 3 4 5 6 7 8 9 10
joy	1 2 3 4 5 6 7 8 9 10
peace	1 2 3 4 5 6 7 8 9 10
patience	1 2 3 4 5 6 7 8 9 10
kindness	1 2 3 4 5 6 7 8 9 10
goodness	1 2 3 4 5 6 7 8 9 10
faithfulness	1 2 3 4 5 6 7 8 9 10
gentleness	1 2 3 4 5 6 7 8 9 10
self-control	1 2 3 4 5 6 7 8 9 10

For more info on **The Big Q: Who is the Holy Spirit, and what does He do?** visit www.dare2share.org/soulfuel/archives and check out *Soul Fuel* question #6.

Ma was proud on my graduation day. I really miss her.

CHAPTER 24

"Heaven Is Nonsmoking, Ma!"

I smoked my first cigarette when I was five years old. Well, okay, it wasn't the whole cigarette; just a few puke-inducing puffs were all I needed to "just say no" to tobacco for good.

Who gave that first cancer stick to me? Dear ol' Ma.

Now before you freak out and think of her as a bad mother, please understand it was her first feeble attempt at drug prevention in my life. And it worked. I never smoked a cigarette or toked a you-know-what because of that experience.

Before that scared-smokeless occasion, I hated cigarettes. This made me hate them even more. My hatred for cigarettes intensified over the years as I grew from a child to a teenager.

I hated the fact that my clothes always smelled like smoke.

I hated the fact that I had to hold my breath every time I walked through our living room so I didn't have to inhale my mom's second-hand choke smoke.

I hated hearing my mom cough so loud and so often in the middle of the night that I had to cover my ears with the pillow so I could sleep.

I hated the fact that my mom was not just a smoker, but a proud smoker. She smoked two packs a day for 54 years. She started smoking when she was 15 and didn't stop until she was dead at 69. Even in hospice I had to scold her for trying to escape and smoke with an oxygen tank strapped over her shoulder and a plastic tube of O^2 shoved up her nostrils. I told her, "Ma, if you are going to die of cancer, die of cancer. Please don't die from lighting a cigarette around an oxygen tank."

When I was 10 and 11 years old, Ma sent me to the local convenience store to buy her some cigarettes. The store clerks almost always sold them to me. I just showed them a handwritten note from my mom that usually said, "Please let my son Greg Stier buy cigarettes from you. I'm at the house and can't get out at this time. Sincerely, Shirley Taylor."

Her handwriting was so beautiful that I think most clerks thought it was legit. Surely a kid couldn't write this beautifully. But if by chance the store clerk asked if the cigarettes were for me, I would lash out, "Do I look like I smoke?" The intensity and volume of my speech made the clerk realize I was buying them under duress and had no interest in smoking.

Ma's smoking is really weird, because she was an absolute health nut, especially when it came to nutrition and vitamins. Every day she loaded herself, me, and my brother up with vitamins to keep us healthy. She would make me take big sips of cod liver oil (not recommended) and mix wheat germ (yes, there is a product with the word *germ* in it) into my food.

When we went into restaurants, she would often grill the waitresses about what was in the food: "Does this have MSG in it?" "Are these peaches canned or fresh?" "Is this bread processed or homemade?"

On and on and on she would go with the questions. It was embarrassing. Finally, in absolute frustration I asked her, "Ma, what do you care? You smoke two packs of cigarettes a day, and you care whether or not these peaches are canned or fresh?"

Bad idea.

The bottom line, whether I liked it or not, was that Ma smoked, and she smoked a lot. In some ways I think it was more than just a physiological addiction. It was a deeply held emotional addiction with her.

If she didn't smoke she'd have nothing to do with her hands, nothing to look forward to in 15 minutes, nothing to distract her from the deep pain inside her soul.

It's almost as though the smoke from her cigarettes became a fog to hide in, a smoke screen where she could be safe. By smoking, with the nicotine sending pulses of endorphins into her veins and throughout her system, she could numb herself from the pain within, the pain of sin, of guilt, of regret.

I'm not going to spend a lot more time on what these sins were (you already know one of them from chapter 1), but rather on the question that haunted my mom for years.

The Big Q: Can I really be forgiven for all my sins, even the really bad ones?

From the time I truly understood the gospel on June 23, 1974, as an eight-year-old boy, until the time I was a teenager, I shared the gospel with my mom again and again. We had the same conversation dozens of times:

"Hey, Ma," I would ask. "Where are you going to go when you die?"

"I hope heaven," she would respond.

"Ma, you can know that you are going to heaven if you believe in Jesus and trust in Him to forgive you for all your sins."

"Greg, you don't know the things I've done wrong. I've done some really bad things in my life."

BLAST FROM THE PAST

No child of God sins to that degree as to make himself incapable of forgiveness.[1]

—JOHN BUNYAN, 17TH CENTURY PREACHER

"Ma, Jesus died for them all, even the really bad ones."

"I hope so."

My brother and I shared the gospel with her many times, but every time she would end up saying how bad she was and that she wasn't sure if God would forgive her.

The Bible makes it clear that God will forgive every sin, even the really bad ones, if we simply trust in Jesus as our Savior. Check out Colossians 2:13-14: "When you were dead in your sins and in the uncircumcision of your sinful nature, God made you alive with Christ. He forgave us all our sins, having canceled the written code, with its regulations, that was against us and that stood opposed to us; he took it away, nailing it to the cross."

Look at the phrase "he forgave us all our sins" for a moment. All of them are forgiven. And what do we know about the forgiveness of God? Check out Jeremiah 31:34: "I will forgive their wickedness and will remember their sins no more."

 INSANE BRAIN STRAIN

If God promises to forgive all our sins, does that mean He forgets them?

Many times when I'm telling someone about the unconditional forgiveness that Jesus offers, he or she asks the question, "What about the blasphemy of the Spirit? Will God forgive that?"

To discover the answer, let's look to the words of Jesus in Matthew 12:31-32: "Every sin and blasphemy will be forgiven men, but the blasphemy against the Spirit will not be forgiven. Anyone who speaks a word against the Son of Man will be forgiven, but anyone who speaks against the Holy Spirit will not be forgiven, either in this age or in the age to come."

Jesus puts it pretty bluntly. The blasphemy of the Spirit will NOT be forgiven. So the next big question is *What is it, and have you committed it?*

To learn the answer to this question you have to understand the context of this passage. The unbelieving Jews of Jesus' time were attacking Him by falsely accusing Him of using demonic spirits to cast out demons. Jesus told them that they weren't really attacking Him, but the Holy Spirit. In other words, they were claiming that the power of the Holy Spirit was demonic. That, my friend, is blasphemy.

But I think that the blasphemy of the Spirit goes deeper still. You see, that same Holy Spirit was convicting the unbelieving Jews of their sins and pointing to Jesus as the true Savior of the world. But instead of repenting (changing their minds) about Jesus, they refused to give in to the Spirit of God. They shut Him out of their souls and cemented their unbelief in blasphemy.

What is blasphemy of the Holy Spirit? I'm convinced that it is the ongoing refusal to give in to the Spirit's promptings pointing to Jesus as the Way, the Truth, and the Life. If people continually refuse to trust in Jesus, they have committed the one unforgivable sin; they have refused to believe in Jesus. Check out Jesus' own words in John 3:18: "Whoever believes in him is not condemned, **but whoever does not believe stands condemned already** because he has not believed in the name of God's one and only Son."

What does this mean for you? If you have put your faith and

trust in Jesus, you cannot commit the blasphemy of the Spirit because you have already broken the chain of unbelief!

Go Figure!

Open your Bible and read 1 John 1:5-10. Answer these questions:

1. What does it mean to "walk in darkness"? How is sinning like walking around in the dark?

   _____

   _____

   _____

2. Do Christians continue to sin after they are saved? Why or why not?

   _____

   _____

   _____

3. What is the condition for forgiveness according to verse 9?

   _____

   _____

   _____

4. What happens when we confess our sins to God?

   _____

   _____

   _____

5. Does He forgive us every time we confess? Why or why not?

_____

_____

_____

6. Does forgiveness depend on how sorry we feel? Why or why not?

_____

_____

_____

So What?

Maybe you were on the brink of having an abortion like my mom . . . or maybe you had one. Or perhaps it's an undying hatred in your heart toward your parents or an insatiable lust or addiction or compulsion that has gotten you bogged down. Do you gossip, steal, lie, or cheat in school? Just remember that if you have put your faith in Jesus, that sin is nailed to the cross. You have been legally justified ("declared to be righteous") in the courtroom of God and have been fully forgiven.

This forgiveness is not a license to sin but a reason to drop down on your knees and worship God with all your soul, strength, mind, and might.

I'll never forget the day in ninth grade when I asked my mom one more time . . .

"Ma, do you know for sure you are going to heaven when you die?"

"I hope so."

"Ma, how many sins did Jesus die for when He died on the cross?"

"All of them, I guess."

"Even the really bad ones, Ma?"

"I don't know, Greg. I've done some pretty bad—"

"Ma, how many sins did Jesus die for?"

"All of them."

I'll never forget what happened next.

"Then if you put your faith and trust in Jesus, where are you going when you die?"

"Heaven!"

"So, Ma, will you trust in Jesus right now to take you to heaven?"

"Yes!"

"Then where are you going when you die?"

"I'm going to heaven, cigarettes and all!"

"But heaven is nonsmoking, Ma!"

"It better not be!"

In that moment, my mom passed out of spiritual death into spiritual life. In spite of her sinful choices as a teenager and young woman, in spite of the fact that she almost aborted me, Jesus forgave all of her sins.

No matter what your past, Jesus can change your future. If you simply put your faith and trust in Jesus, your sins (the past, present, and future ones) are wiped away for good. Do it now, and then ask everyone you know to do the same!

YOU'RE NEXT!

Satan loves to make Christians believe we really aren't forgiven and that we should feel guilty all the time, but we don't have to listen to him. Take some time and list the sins from the past that still haunt you (use a separate paper if you want to keep the list private), then beside each one, write FORGIVEN and FORGOTTEN! Then the next time Satan tries to put you on a guilt trip, open this page or piece of paper and remind yourself that Jesus has forgiven your sins and forgotten them, too.

_____

_____

_____

_____

_____

_____

_____

_____

_____

_____

_____

_____

_____

* * *

For more info on The Big Q: Can I really be forgiven for all my sins, even the really bad ones? visit www.dare2share.org/soulfuel/ archives and check out *Soul Fuel* question #18.

CHAPTER 25

Death Encounter #4: Massive Heart Attack

I will never forget it. It came suddenly. My heart was immediately seized with searing pain, the kind that I had never felt before or since. It sent chills rushing throughout my paralyzed body.

What was it? The news that my grandpa had just had a massive heart attack.

This was my final encounter with death during the early years of my life and it was the hardest to take.

I could take going through a window, choking on a piece of butterscotch candy, being attacked by demonic dogs, and having my appendix burst. But what I couldn't deal with was losing my grandpa.

He hung on in ICU for two weeks. I went to the hospital night after night, watching my big, tough uncles reduced to red eyes and tears as they waited for the inevitable.

It was hard to watch my strong, strapping grandpa struggle for every labored breath. It was heartbreaking to see his eyeballs roll back into his head and his eyelids twitch and flutter randomly.

Grandma told me later that all the rolling and twitching stopped when she was leaving his hospital room late one night. She heard a loud gasp and turned around to see my grandpa alive for one last millisecond. In that flash she witnessed his last moment on this side of eternity. She said that he was sitting straight up with his arms stretched upward. His eyes were no longer rolling back but riveted on one point. She said it was as though he could see straight through the ceiling to the open arms of the Savior in heaven waiting to receive him. He then collapsed back into the hospital bed and died, with an ever so slight smile on his face.

I'll never forget getting called one last time to go and see my grandpa's body. I say it this way, because my grandpa was gone. He was safely in the arms of his Savior.

When I realized for the first time that I wouldn't see him again on this side of eternity, I broke down and cried as I don't remember ever crying before.

This death encounter hit me hard. And the question that often hovers around the death of loved ones made its way into my mind: *Why?* Why did Grandpa have to die at the relatively young age of 68? Why couldn't I have more time with the man I respected so much? Why would God take him when my grandma needed him so much? These questions and a hundred more swirled around in my brain for hours, days, and weeks after Grandpa passed away. The only thing they had in common was that they started with the same word: *Why?*

The Big Q: Why did Jesus die on the cross?

I'm sure that the disciples and friends of Jesus were asking the same thing when He was wrongly arrested in the Garden of Gethsemane and marched through six "court proceedings" in the middle of the night. I'm sure that as Peter watched from a distance as Jesus was pummeled again and again by angry fists he was asking *why?*

To begin with, Jesus didn't deserve to die. He was God in the flesh and He had never sinned, not even once. He was the most perfect being ever to walk the planet.

But not only did Jesus die, He was beaten beyond recognition by angry Roman soldiers.

They stripped Him, tied Him up, and then tortured Him beyond our worst nightmares. They took a whip nicknamed a cat-o'-nine-tails and flung into His exposed back, buttocks, and legs again and again and again, until His exposed body was nothing more than shredded ribbons of flesh, muscle, and sinew.

What's weird is that He could have stopped it at any time. Just remember who we are talking about here. It's Jesus . . . the God-man, the maker of heaven and earth, the one who spoke everything in this universe into existence, the supreme ruler of the universe.

I'm reminded of what Jesus told Peter in Matthew 26:53 when Peter tried to prevent the officials from arresting Jesus. Jesus asked, "Do you think I cannot call on my Father, and he will at once put at my disposal more than twelve legions of angels?" There were 5,000 soldiers in each Roman legion at the time. So Jesus is reminding Peter that He could call on God and He would send 60,000 warrior angels to set Him free. But that was not the plan. The plan was that Jesus would suffer and die for the sins of all humanity.

BLAST FROM THE PAST

Learn to know Christ and him crucified. Learn to sing to him, and say, "Lord Jesus, you are my righteousness, I am your sin. You have taken upon yourself what is mine and given me what is yours. You have become what you were not so that I might become what I was not."[1]

—MARTIN LUTHER, 16TH CENTURY CHURCH REFORMER

They beat a crown of thorns into His skull, spat in His face, and mocked Him relentlessly. But that was just the beginning.

They marched Him up a hill outside Jerusalem called Golgotha. There the Roman soldiers nailed Jesus to a cross with three spike nails. He hung naked, twisted, tortured, and dying for six painfully long hours. With each labored breath, His body pushed up to exhale and down to inhale. Breathing became His torture chamber. Every time He pushed up to breathe, His exposed nerves scraped against the rough bark of the old rugged cross and lightning bolts of raw pain shot through His mangled and broken body.

Why?

Why the Son of God? Why such a horrible death for such an amazing person?

Even Jesus screamed out why with His words, "Eloi, Eloi, *lama sabachthani?*" which means, "My God, My God, why have you forsaken me?" (Matthew 27:46).

INSANE BRAIN STRAIN

Why did Jesus have to be brutally tortured and executed? Couldn't He have paid for sin without having to suffer so badly?

The dejected disciples lacked the courage to stand against those who sought to arrest Jesus. They were probably confused by Jesus' seeming obsession with dying (He had been mentioning it a lot). They were shocked that He didn't seem to be the Messiah they had been hoping for, the Messiah who would overthrow Roman rule and establish His kingdom on earth. Instead He was the one who was overwhelmed by Roman fists, whips, wood, and nails.

Why?
Luke 24:13-21, 25-27, 31-32 addresses this question.

Now that same day two of them were going to a village called
Emmaus, about seven miles from Jerusalem. They were talking
with each other about everything that had happened. As they
talked and discussed these things with each other, Jesus himself
came up and walked along with them; but they were kept from
recognizing him.

He asked them, "What are you discussing together as you
walk along?"

They stood still, their faces downcast. One of them,
named Cleopas, asked him, "Are you only a visitor to Jerusalem
and do not know the things that have happened there in these
days?"

"What things?" he asked.

"About Jesus of Nazareth," they replied. "He was a prophet,
powerful in word and deed before God and all the people. The
chief priests and our rulers handed him over to be sentenced to
death, and they crucified him; but we had hoped that he was the
one who was going to redeem Israel.". . .

He said to them, "How foolish you are, and how slow of
heart to believe all that the prophets have spoken! Did not the
Christ have to suffer these things and then enter his glory?" And
beginning with Moses and all the Prophets, he explained to
them what was said in all the Scriptures concerning himself. . . .

Then their eyes were opened and they recognized him. . . .
They asked each other, "Were not our hearts burning within us
while he talked with us on the road and opened the Scriptures
to us?"

Why were their hearts burning? Because the resurrected Jesus had explained to them from the Old Testament why He had to die on the cross and rise again. They had been hoping that the Messiah would be a ruling king, but instead He came as a suffering servant. But through His suffering, the sin of humanity was paid for once for all.

Go Figure!

Open your Bible and read Psalm 22:1-19.

Psalm 22 is written from the perspective of Jesus as He hung on the cross—but written 1,000 years before it happened! Read verses 1-19 again and imagine what Jesus went through. Answer the following questions:

1. What do you learn about Jesus from these verses?

_____

_____

_____

2. Why did He cry out to God, asking, "Why have you forsaken me"?

_____

_____

_____

3. Did Jesus suffer more from physical or emotional pain? Why?

_____

_____

_____

4. If you were hanging on the cross next to Jesus, what would you say to Him?

_____

_____

_____

5. How does it make you feel knowing that Jesus took your place on the cross?

_____

_____

_____

6. How should His death on the cross impact your day-to-day life?

_____

_____

_____

Remember the poison of sin from chapter 4? It had spread to every person in the human race through the sin of Adam. But through the obedience of Jesus dying on the cross, the antidote is available in the blood of Jesus.

I love the words of Romans 3:23-25: "All have sinned and fall short of the glory of God, and are justified freely by his grace through the redemption that came by Christ Jesus. God presented him as a sacrifice of atonement, through faith in his blood."

We all have been poisoned by sin, but Jesus took that poison onto Himself when He died on the cross and died in our place for our sin. The antidote He offered is permanent. Once we taste of it, we no longer are destined for death, but eternal life. How do we receive the antidote? We ingest it through faith. We believe, and we receive.

A great Old Testament passage pushes the poison analogy a little further. It tells of the Israelites being overrun by poisonous snakes while under the judgment of God in the desert. Moses pleaded with God to save the Israelites. Here are God's instructions in Numbers 21:8-9: "The LORD said to Moses, 'Make a snake and put it up on a pole; anyone who is bitten can look at it and live.' So Moses made a bronze snake and put it up on a pole. Then when anyone was bitten by a snake and looked at the bronze snake, he lived."

Sounds kind of weird. God basically tells Moses that the antidote to the poisonous snakebites is found in taking a fake snake made of bronze, sticking it up on a pole, and telling people to look at it. But we know now that this weird exercise was all pointing forward to the death of Jesus on a pole of sorts.

Later on in John 3:14-15, Jesus used this Old Testament story to describe His crucifixion on the cross: "Just as Moses lifted up the snake in the desert, so the Son of Man must be lifted up, that everyone who believes in him may have eternal life."

What's the point? All you must do is look and live, look to Jesus and live forever. If Jesus hadn't died on the cross, none of this would have been possible . . . but He did, and so now we can believe and receive, believe in Him, and receive the gift of eternal life.

So What?

That should be obvious. If you haven't trusted in Jesus alone to forgive you for your sin and give you eternal life, now is the time.

Look and live. Do it now.

If you have already trusted in Jesus, then take your friends who have been poisoned by the venomous snakes of sin and point them to Jesus, hanging on the cross, who died so they could look and live.

When my grandpa died, I had the privilege of presenting the gospel at his funeral. Out of the hundreds that came to say good-bye to my grandpa that day, scores said hello to Jesus.

Why?

Because I held up the cross of Jesus in my talk and begged them to look and live. So many did that day, my heart rejoiced.

YOU'RE NEXT!

Take some time and write out a prayer or a poem of thanksgiving to Jesus for what He went through and accomplished for us on the cross.

_____

_____

_____

_____

_____

_____

_____

_____

_____

_____

_____

_____

✳ ✳ ✳

For more info on **The Big Q: Why did Jesus die on the cross?** visit www.dare2share.org/soulfuel/archives and check out *Soul Fuel* question #4.

CHAPTER 26

One Rogue Uncle

My hands were shaking and my heart was pounding as I walked to the pulpit in the tiny mortuary. Hundreds had gathered for Grandpa's funeral. As a 15-year-old kid looking at the crowd and preparing to speak, I should have been nervous about my presentation, but the thoughts making my heart race were about Uncle Richard.

He was my one uncle who wasn't open to the gospel message. Like my other uncles, he was tough as nails and wasn't afraid to get in a brawl. I had heard stories of the fights he had been in growing up. My family told me about the time he jumped through the passenger-side window of a moving car full of tough guys who were out to get Richard and his brothers. He took all of them on as the car wove back and forth down the road. Two blocks later, the car finally crashed, giving my other uncles time to catch up with the now wrecked vehicle and give Richard some backup.

One by one, the others had come to Christ. The other tough guys wilted under the sheer power of the gospel message. A spiritual outbreak infected my entire family—except for Uncle Richard. He seemed immune to the message.

Whenever one of my uncles brought up the gospel, he would shut them down. He was happy with his personal beliefs and didn't want my uncles to force their beliefs on him. We all grieved for Richard. That's why we hoped he would respond to the gospel at my grandpa's funeral. We hoped Grandfather's death would get Uncle Richard thinking about eternity.

At Grandpa's funeral, as I presented the gospel and gave the "bow your heads and raise your hands" invitation to respond, I looked toward my one rogue uncle. But his arms stayed down, his heart hardened in spiritual concrete.

Soon after I wrote a letter to Uncle Richard and expressed how much I hoped he would become a Christian. He never responded. Not a phone call. Not a postcard. Nothing. What could I do? He wouldn't talk about it with me, his brothers, or anyone for that matter. We could do nothing else except pray and wonder.

Uncle Richard's situation filled my mind with all sorts of questions: "What about people who are really sincere in what they believe? Will they make it to heaven?"

"Are there situations where God will make exceptions to His rule that salvation comes by faith in Jesus alone?"

"What about people who are superdedicated to their particular religion—will they make it in?"

Then I began to realize that the answers to the questions were almost as frightening as the questions themselves.

The Big Q: If Jesus is the only way to heaven, are all other religions wrong?

Jesus made it crystal clear in John 14:6 that He is the Way, the Truth, and the Life and that nobody comes to the Father except through Him. The implications of this bold statement are obvious. If Jesus is the only way, then all the other ways are simply wrong.

This would mean that Muslims, Buddhists, Hindus, anyone and everyone who doesn't put his or her faith in Jesus alone is headed for an eternity without Christ, an eternity of flames.

Whoa! Scary stuff.

But we don't make the rules, God does. His rules rule.

I talk to teens all the time who assume that what they believe dictates reality. They say stuff like, "Well, I know you believe that Jesus is the only way to heaven, but I don't believe that, so I'll be all right."

Usually my response goes something like, "So if there is a tornado outside that is closing in on your house but you don't believe it, then are you safe?" That's when they usually start getting the point.

Our beliefs don't create or control reality. Remember what truth is? It is what is. It is real, raw reality, whether we like it or not, whether we believe it or not. Let me give you some more examples:

You've run out of gas but you don't believe it.

You failed to write a report but refuse to believe that your teacher will fail you.

You've snapped your leg in a basketball game and can see the bone sticking through the skin, but you choose not to recognize the reality that the bone is broken.

Does any amount of belief change the reality of any of these situations? In the same way, if Jesus is the Way, the Truth, and the Life, then all religions that don't recognize this are flat-out wrong. It doesn't matter how sincere people are or how much they believe in

> **BLAST FROM THE PAST**
>
> Also they teach that men cannot be justified before God by their own strength, merits, or works, but are freely justified for Christ's sake, through faith, when they believe that they are received into favor, and that their sins are forgiven for Christ's sake, who, by His death, has made satisfaction for our sins. This faith God imputes for righteousness in His sight.[1]
>
> —Augsburg Confession, 16th century

their creed. As Yankee used to remind us, "Sincerity is no substitute for truth."

Jesus put it this way in Matthew 7:13-23:

> "Enter through the narrow gate. For wide is the gate and broad is the road that leads to destruction, and many enter through it. But small is the gate and narrow the road that leads to life, and only a few find it.
>
> "Watch out for false prophets. They come to you in sheep's clothing, but inwardly they are ferocious wolves. By their fruit you will recognize them. Do people pick grapes from thornbushes, or figs from thistles? Likewise every good tree bears good fruit, but a bad tree bears bad fruit. A good tree cannot bear bad fruit, and a bad tree cannot bear good fruit. Every tree that does not bear good fruit is cut down and thrown into the fire. Thus, by their fruit you will recognize them.
>
> "Not everyone who says to me, 'Lord, Lord,' will enter the kingdom of heaven, but only he who does the will of my Father who is in heaven. Many will say to me on that day, 'Lord, Lord, did we not prophesy in your name, and in your name drive out demons and perform many miracles?' Then I will tell them plainly, 'I never knew you. Away from me, you evildoers!' "

In this unsettling passage, Jesus reminded His followers that the way into heaven is narrow and the way to hell is big and broad. Notice what He says about the false teachers. They look like sheep, they talk like sheep, but down deep inside they are ferocious wolves. Who are these wolves? They are the religious people who say "Lord! Lord!" and claim to speak in the name of the Lord and do miracles— but they never down deep inside did the heavenly Father's will. What is the Father's will? Jesus tells us in John 6:40, "My Father's will is that everyone who looks to the Son and believes in him shall have eternal life, and I will raise him up at the last day."

Those who look, act, and talk like sheep outwardly but inwardly don't look to Jesus and trust in Him alone will hear the dreaded words, "I never knew you. Away from me, you evildoers!"

It doesn't matter what people's religion, sincerity, good deeds, or heroic acts are; if they have not trusted in Jesus alone for their source of salvation, those people are lost and going to hell.

Go Figure!

Read Matthew 23:25-28 and answer these questions:

1. Since the word *woe* is a pronouncement of judgment, how does Jesus feel about the religious Pharisees of His day?

   _____

   _____

   _____

2. Why does He feel this way about them?

   _____

   _____

   _____

3. How does He describe their external appearances and the true condition of their hearts and souls?

   _____

   _____

   _____

4. What does this tell us about Jesus and how He sees many of those whom we perceive as "holy" because they look "religious"?

_____

_____

_____

5. According to Jesus' own prescriptions in other passages, what is the best way to "clean the inside of the cup"?

_____

_____

_____

6. Have you cleaned the inside of your cup?

_____

_____

_____

My uncle Richard was lost, and my other uncles and I all knew it. I had tried. My uncles had tried. We were at the end of our ropes. So we prayed. It was out of our hands. It was always out of our hands, but now we knew it. It would take an act of God to save Richard's hardened soul.

Almost 12 years later, Richard was coming to town again for another memorial service of sorts . . . his own. He had cancer throughout his once healthy, buff, and chiseled body. This deadly disease had spread throughout his organs. He flew back to have one last family reunion and say good-bye to those he loved.

But we were determined to see him again—in eternity. When

Uncle Richard came, however, he made it clear that he didn't want anyone talking about God, sin, or salvation. Instead, he just wanted us to have a good time laughing, talking, and telling stories. In one final, last-ditch effort, my uncle Bob talked him into coming to Grace Church to hear me preach. Richard was hesitant to attend at first, but he finally agreed.

I'll never forget the sight. My uncles, aunts, and cousins were all crammed into the two last pews. These huge muscle-bound believers had only one thing on their minds: Richard's salvation. They prayed the whole service, because they knew that at the end of my sermon I would give the gospel.

After explaining the message of salvation as clearly as I knew how, I asked the people to bow their heads and close their eyes. I asked those who had trusted in Christ as their Savior for the first time to raise a hand. Without a moment's hesitation, Richard and his wife thrust their hands into the air. I could hear the sobs of my family (they had been peeking). The hardened concrete that encased Uncle Richard's heart had finally disintegrated.

 INSANE BRAIN STRAIN
Why did God make the only way into heaven so narrow?

At the airport later that day Richard pulled Bob aside and put his arm around him. "Today I trusted in Jesus Christ," he said. "You're going to see me in heaven someday." Bob wrapped his arms around Richard's frail frame and wept. They said good-bye for the last time, knowing the next time they would see each other would be in heaven's glory.

During the last days of his life, Uncle Richard wanted others to hear the good news of salvation. He asked me to speak at his memorial service in Arizona so the friends he had been witnessing to would have another opportunity to trust in Christ. I agreed.

On August 24, 1995, Richard Mathias met his Savior. After more than 50 years of life on earth Richard finally breathed his last. He opened his eyes in the blaze of heaven's glory moments later. And all because a group of bodybuilding brothers refused to stop praying for the impossible.

Jesus is the Way, the Truth, and the Life. Nobody, not Uncle Richard, not your sincere aunt, not that tribal chief from deep in the jungle, goes to heaven except through Him.

So What?

Get sharpened up on what you believe. Be able to unleash the power of God's Word; present thoughtful questions and penetrating insights to your friends who don't know Jesus. Do everything in your power to convince them that Jesus is the only way—that there is good news! Love them. Serve them. Pursue and persuade them. But above all else, pray for them. Even if it takes 12 years, it's worth it.

YOU'RE NEXT!

Take some time and make up a list of 5 to 10 discussion questions that would help you get a conversation going about Jesus' being the only way. Here are a few to get you started. On a side note, if you don't know the answers to these questions, get together with your youth leader and talk about it. You can also join a message board at www.dare2share.org to engage in discussion.

Do you think all religions basically teach the same thing? Why or why not?

_____

_____

_____

_____

_____

If all religions contradict each other, can they all be right? Why or why not?

_____

_____

_____

_____

_____

Is it arrogant to say that Jesus is the only way? Why or why not?

_____

_____

_____

_____

_____

⁎ ⁎ ⁎

For more info on **The Big Q: If Jesus is the only way to heaven, are
all other religions wrong?** visit www.dare2share.org/soulfuel/archives
and check out *Soul Fuel* question #13.

Believe it or not, big hair was in when I was in high school.

CHAPTER 27

Puppy Love, Broken Hearts, and the Trinity

Kristi was the first girl to catch my eye and break my heart. There were almost four years between those two incidents. The 48 months of "middle time" were mostly a great big mess created by me.

You see, back in high school I was a talker (shouldn't surprise you) and a stalker (may surprise you). Maybe "stalker" is too strong a word, because I wasn't hanging around in the bushes, watching her from a distance. I wasn't a dangerous stalker, just an obnoxious one. Once I set my mind on something or someone, I don't give up until I accomplish my goal. This kind of obsessive focus and effort doesn't always bode well in the relationship arena.

Note to the guys only: Hey, guys, take it from me: Don't be too overanxious to get that one "special girl" at any cost. For one reson it could, and probably will, cost you (and I'm not talking metaphorically). Second, once a girl knows that you *really* like her, she can make use of that information to make you, break you, take you, and shake you. Third, if a girl thinks you like her but could live without her, then she may be much more attracted to you.

Oh, how I wish I would have known these three things in high school. All I knew was that Greg liked Kristi and that someday she would like me back.

I'll never forget calling her up one day and telling her that I was coming over to her house to give her something. She made it clear that, while she "liked me as a friend" (the death-knell statement for future dates, by the way), she would not be home if I came over.

But I decided to go anyway. The problem is that she lived seven miles away, and I had only a skateboard and a backpack full of unwavering determination and stupidity. I skated and skated and skated and skated and skated on a hot summer day, finally making it to her house. When I got there, you guessed it: Kristi wasn't home. So I dropped my little gift with her sister at the door, turned around, and skated and skated and skated and skated and skated back home.

But after a few years of desperate and failed attempts to win her love, the miraculous happened. One day, out of the blue, Kristi fell for me.

Those few months of relational bliss were the culmination of years of prayer, persistence, and persuasion. All the pain seemed worth it at that point. She was in love with me and I with her. We went on dates, had long talks, and went on horseback rides in the back trails by her kinda-out-in-the-boonies neighborhood.

Everything was going great until that one day I got a "Dear Greg" letter. Kristi dumped me. She gave some crazy reason that made no sense to me whatsoever. When I read that letter I ran out into a rainstorm, fell into a great big mud puddle, and cried for what seemed like hours. I'm sure it looked like some kind of scene out of a horrible B movie, the distraught rejected boyfriend covered in mud, screaming up into the sky, "Why, God? Why me? Why? Why? Why?" Imagine the most melodramatic, pitiful scene you can imagine . . . and then multiply by 10.

Not my crowning moment.

My friends had to put me in the shower so I wouldn't get the mud that was dripping from my body all over the floor. I just cried and cried and cried. My friends tried to console and counsel me, but I would not be comforted.

My heart had been broken as it had never been broken before—and now I thank God for it.

The months that followed transformed me forever. How? They made me seek the Trinity with all of my heart, soul, mind, and might. I prayed something like, "God, if You don't reveal Yourself to me, Your whole self to me, during this time, I don't think I can make it through this."

He did. I did.

That year helped me to know God as I had never known Him before. I learned more about the Father, Son, and Holy Spirit. I discovered the power of the Trinity—the completeness of God. And, what surprised me the most, was I found the love that I had been so longing for. The love that I thought I wanted from Kristi was waiting for me at the epicenter of God.

The Big Q: What is the Trinity?

The Trinity is the Christian belief that while there is only one true God, He exists in the form of three distinct persons: the Father, the Son, and the Holy Spirit. The word *Trinity* is a combination of *tri* meaning "three" (like *tri*cycle) and *unity* meaning "one." Put those together you have the basic idea "three-oneness."

Get it?

Neither do I! To be honest, the truth about the Trinity makes my brain hurt.

There are certain things I will never understand, like quantum physics, Mandarin Chinese, and guys who wear pink. But these three hard-to-understand subjects pale in comparison to the mystery of the Trinity.

Even though trying to comprehend the Trinity is like attempting to drink the ocean, we should at least try a gulp. So here it goes.

The basic definition of the Trinity is a word used to express the doctrine of the unity of God as subsisting in three distinct Persons.

Oh, that helps.

Somebody tried to use an egg to describe the Trinity. An egg has three parts, but it is still one egg. The problem is that the yolk is not the shell, and the shell is not the white, and the Trinity is not an omelet.

Others have said the Trinity is like H_2O (if you failed science, it's also called "water"). H_2O can come in liquid, solid, and gas forms. The liquid one we drink, the solid one (ice) we put in our drinks, and the gaseous form we call steam. They are three different forms but the same ingredients. But this illustration falls short, too.

> **BLAST FROM THE PAST**
> As well might a gnat seek to drink in the ocean, as a finite creature to comprehend the Eternal God.[1]
> —CHARLES SPURGEON, 19TH CENTURY PREACHER

As a matter of fact, no human analogy equates. The Trinity is beyond the scope of human comprehension. But if we truly believe the Bible, we must accept the truth of the Trinity even if we can't begin to understand it.

This really shouldn't be a problem, because we do the same thing all the time, don't we? We accept realities that we don't understand. Stop for a moment and think about your brain. You don't really know *how* your brain works, do you? But you probably accept the reality *that* it works. If you can do that with the three pounds of wormy-looking gray mass stuck between your ears, then maybe you can do that with the God of the universe.

Although the word *Trinity* is never found in the Bible, the concept is all over its pages. From page one, verse one, we see it: "In the beginning God created the heavens and the earth." In Hebrew, the original language of the Old Testament, this statement has a singular noun and a plural verb (in other words one, yet more!). Verses later God says, "Let **us** make man in **our** image." It seems as though God is talking to Himself because He is! Right from the start of the Bible we get to sit in on a roundtable discussion on the Father, Son, and Holy Spirit!

INSANE BRAIN STRAIN

The concept of the Trinity is that there is one God who exists in the form of three separate yet equal Persons. How would you explain this to someone who has heard of the Trinity but doesn't know how to defend the idea? Guess what? In the "You're Next!" section, you get a chance to do this!

From Genesis through Revelation, the Trinity is absolutely unavoidable. We serve one God who exists in the form of three persons. We see it in the Great Commission when Jesus said we should baptize disciples "in the **name** of the Father, Son, and Holy Spirit." He didn't say "names," but "name." One Name, one God, three persons.

We also see it in verses like Matthew 3:16-17: "As soon as Jesus was baptized, he went up out of the water. At that moment heaven was opened, and he saw the Spirit of God descending like a dove and lighting on him. And a voice from heaven said, 'This is my Son, whom I love; with him I am well pleased.' "

In these two verses you experience the three different persons involved in the Trinity. You see Jesus and the Spirit of God in the form of a dove. You also hear the voice of God the Father. What you also experience, by the way, is a whole lot of love. The Father says this of His Son Jesus: "This is my Son, whom I love; with him I am well pleased." There is an unfathomable love that the members of the Trinity have for each other—but more on that later.

When you compare these two verses to Isaiah 43:10-11, the truth of the Trinity becomes undeniable: " 'You are my witnesses,' declares the LORD, 'and my servant whom I have chosen, so that you may know and believe me and understand that I am he. Before me no god was formed, nor will there be one after me. I, even I, am the LORD, and apart from me there is no savior.' "

This passage makes it clear that there is only one God, and the Matthew verses show us that this one God exists in the form of three persons—the Trinity.

Let's take a look at each of the three unique members of this amazing God that we serve.

- The Father (the invisible initiator who sits in an "unapproachable light," according to 1 Timothy 6:16, and who is in complete control of everything that unfolds in this universe)
- The Son (the person of God in human form, aka "The Son of Man," who does the Father's will without hesitation)
- The Holy Spirit (the unseen member of the Trinity who supports and executes the agenda of both the Father and the Son!)

These members are each fully God but are three unique persons! They are always on the same page, always in complete harmony, always working together, always executing the divine agenda in powerful ways to bring maximum glory to God! They never had a beginning and never had a disagreement. Although we can't see the Father (1 Timothy 6:16), we will see the Son someday (1 Timothy 6:14) and can feel the effect of the Spirit in our lives every day (Ephesians 5:18).

Does your brain hurt yet?

Go Figure!

Read John 1:1-4 and verses 14-18, and then answer these questions:

1. How can the "Word" be "with God" and be God at the same time?

   _____

   _____

   _____

2. What does the fact that "the Word" created the universe tell you about how much power He has?

   _____

   _____

   _____

3. What does the reality that true life is found in Him tell you about who He may be?

   _____

   _____

   _____

4. Does verse 14 confirm or contradict who you think "the Word" may be?

   _____

   _____

   _____

5. According to verse 18, who is the only one to have ever seen the Father?

_____

_____

_____

6. How do you see at least part of the truth of the Trinity in verse 18?

_____

_____

_____

So What?

If your brain doesn't hurt yet, stop and think about this for a minute: The truth of the Trinity is immensely relevant and encouraging. How? It reminds us that we are never alone. In the midst of school and sports and life there is a whole team, Team Trinity, with you. You never sit at your school cafeteria table alone. The Father is right across from you to hear your prayers, the Son is at His right hand to defend you from a bully named Satan, and the Holy Spirit is sitting right next to you to encourage you, coach you, and strengthen you.

Jesus put it this way in John 14: "If you love me, you will obey what I command. And I will ask the Father, and he will give you another Counselor to be with you forever—the Spirit of truth. The world cannot accept him, because it neither sees him nor knows him. But you know him, for he lives with you and will be in you."

The Father, Son, and Holy Spirit are in you and around you right now. You are not alone. You are never alone. You never will be alone.

So talk to God with reckless abandon. Enter the circle of the Trinity's friendship. God is inviting you into His most intimate interactions. You have an invitation to intimacy with the Father, Son, and Holy Spirit. Jesus prayed this about us in John 17:20-21: "My prayer is . . . that all of them may be one, Father, just as you are in me and I am in you. **May they also be in us so that the world may believe that you have sent me.**"

When we begin to enjoy our relationship with the Trinity, the world can't help but sit up and take notice. People will see the Father, Son, and Holy Spirit's power, love, and grace unleashed in, around, and through us.

What will the Trinity do for you? The Trinity will invite you into a love relationship. The Trinity will heal your broken heart. The Trinity will never send you a "Dear John" or "Dear Jordan" letter. The Trinity will never leave you, forsake you, or break up with you.

Take it from me. A few years after I broke up with Kristi I met my human soul mate, the second love of my life, Debbie. We dated for four years and, at the time of this writing, have been married for 15 years.

And who was the first real love of my life? Kristi? No. It's the Trinity. As much as I love my wife, my kids, and my friends, these loves pale in comparison to the love I feel for God. And the love I feel for God pales in comparison to the love He feels for me . . . and for you.

If all this stuff gives you a headache, then take an aspirin. Take one pill at three separate times if you need too. But even if the Trinity makes our brains hurt, it should make our hearts sing!

YOU'RE NEXT!

Respond with two or three paragraphs to a friend who sent you this e-mail:

Hey!

Some religious people just came to my door and started telling me that the Trinity doesn't exist. They had verses and stuff to back it up, and after 15 minutes or so I was ready to believe them. But then I remembered when I went to the Dare 2 Share conference with you that crazy speaker guy talked about how the Trinity does exist . . . so now I'm really confused! What do you think? Who is right? Do you know what the Bible really teaches? And most important, what does it matter if we believe in the Trinity or not? Help!

_____

_____

_____

_____

_____

_____

_____

_____

_____

_____

_____

✳ ✳ ✳

For more info on **The Big Q: What is the Trinity?** visit www.dare 2share.org/soulfuel/archives and check out *Soul Fuel* question #2.

CHAPTER 28

Run! Run! Granny's Got a Gun!

Affter my grandpa died, my poor grandma was traumatized. For five decades Grandma and Grandpa had been at each other's side. So when Grandpa died, there was a huge hole in her soul. (She had secretly married him when she was 16. For a while her parents didn't know anything about it. Finally their marriage went public, and they moved in together. Back in the old days weird things like that happened all the time.)

To add insult to injury, my grandma became potential prey for a whole lot of crooks and criminals who loved to take advantage of little old ladies. Many of these charlatans assumed that these deceased husbands left their grieving widows miles and piles of cash. All they wanted to do was help these wonderful grannies "manage" their finances, with the money managing to end up in the crooks' wallets.

Although by this time my grandma lived in the suburbs, she had lived in the roughest part of the city for decades. She may have looked like an innocent old lady, but Grandma had street smarts. She could usually smell a con from a mile away.

One day after my grandpa died, she got a call from a salesman who wanted to meet with Grandma about a medical alert system. The whole idea, he said, was that if she was having a medical emergency, all she had to do was push a button, and the ambulance would show up at her door.

The man, who seemed nice enough on the phone, set up an appointment with my grandma and told her he couldn't wait to show her his breakthrough product in person.

My grandmother became wary when the appointment time came and went. One hour, then two hours, and, finally three hours passed by the time the salesman finally showed up. The problem was that by this time Grandma had already locked and loaded a gun. She had caught the scent of a con, and her gun was ready, just in case.

She greeted the salesman at the door and let him into the house. Grandma sat him down at the kitchen table, casually pulled out the large pistol, and calmly laid it on the table.

The poor salesman turned pale. He asked haltingly, "What's that for, ma'am?"

"It's for you, if you are not for real," Grandma replied.

"What do you mean?" the man asked, beads of perspiration quickly gathering on his brow.

"Well, I'm a widow, and there are a lot of charlatans out there trying to take advantage of nice, little old ladies like me, so I just wanted to show you my gun. It is a loaded .357 Magnum, and I know how to use it. I used to win shooting competitions, you know. If you are legitimate, you have nothing to worry about. But if you are trying to rip me off and take my money, I will shoot you right where you sit."

Grandma said it coolly and casually, like she was ordering from a menu.

The man panicked and blurted, "Ma'am, I'm going to get sick."

"Don't worry, honey," she said, picking up the revolver and holding it up for him to see. "If you are legit, I won't kill you. Would it help if I took the gun and held it under the table?"

"I have got to go before I throw up!" the man replied, running out of the house.

Now to this day I don't know if the guy was legit or a fake, but one thing I do know, Grandma wasn't fake. As hard as it is to believe today in our politically correct culture, Grandma wielding a gun on this unsuspecting salesman or criminal wasn't a surprise to any of us in the family.

Why? Because our family had lots and lots of guns . . . and not all of them were for hunting. When I was five years old, Grandma taught me how to shoot in case somebody broke into our house, intending us bodily harm. She told me where the guns were, how to use them, and why it was important to "shoot to kill."

To be honest, it all kind of freaked me out and scared me. But Grandma always assured me that these guns were to be used for defensive purposes only, as a last resort, if somebody was trying to hurt me or my family.

I don't know how you feel about guns, and I don't quite know how I feel about them either, but Granny was probably overdoing it. (I've done too many funerals for too many teens who have been accidentally shot playing around with them.) But I do know this: From the time I was young my family drilled into my head that guns were to be used for defensive purposes only.

What's true of guns is also true of using facts, evidences, and verses when we are defending our faith. Too many times as a teenager, I loaded them like ammo in my gospel gun so that I could "blow away" the Mormon, Wiccan, atheist, or whoever had made his or her way into my spiritual sights.

I remember once when I was in high school that I argued with a group of Mormons for two full hours in a local shopping mall. They had their ammo, and I had my ammo. Although my ammo was better (because it was based on Scripture), ultimately it felt like I was shooting blanks. Why? Because I had viewed this whole encounter as a shoot-out rather than a conversation!

Over and over I made this mistake in my junior high and high school years until I began to realize that the old adage was true: "You can't argue somebody into heaven." Having the best ammo and the biggest gun doesn't necessarily mean that you'll win when it comes to sharing the message of Jesus.

The Big Q: How do I defend my faith?

When it comes to defending your faith it is vitally important not to be offensive. Rule number one is that if you are not loving toward others, then they may not be loving toward you. If you are rude, sarcastic, and condescending to others, then, chances are, they will be the same toward you.

This means listening, asking thoughtful questions, and treating others respectfully, no matter how far out their beliefs are. It also means trying to discover what others believe before ramming and cramming your beliefs down their throats.

One of the biggest lessons I have learned (and am still learning) is that the more you show the love of Jesus, the more the walls come down. The more the walls come down, the more likely people are to listen. When someone feels listened to and understood, all those defense mechanisms that shield his or her heart and mind begin to crack. Once these walls are down and the two of you are having a real conversation, that's when the facts, the verses, and truths of God's Word can be useful.

INSANE BRAIN STRAIN

How do I defend my faith without being defensive . . . especially when I'm being told that I'm wrong?

Maybe that's why I love James 1:19 so much: "My dear brothers, take note of this: Everyone should be quick to listen, slow to speak and slow to become angry."

There are two reminders in this passage that can help us, not just in defending our faith, but in all of our daily interactions with others.

1. Be quick to listen and slow to speak.

There's an old adage that goes, "God gave us two ears and one mouth for a reason. We should be listening twice as much as we talk." For some of us, that comes much easier. For some of us, that comes with much more difficulty. You'll have no problem guessing which one I am.

If you are the type who listens more than you talk, that is great! Keep it up. Just don't forget that, after all your listening, the goal is to share with that person the good news

BLAST FROM THE PAST

Reason is a property of God's, since there is nothing which God, the creator of all things, has not foreseen, arranged and determined by reason; moreover, there is nothing He does not wish to be investigated and understood by reason.[1]

—TERTULLIAN, 3RD CENTURY THEOLOGIAN

of Jesus. If you are more inclined to talk first, talk often, and talk some more after that, get in the habit of disciplining yourself to ask questions (a form of talking) and then letting the other people share what they believe with no running commentary from you.

It may feel awkward at first, but believe me, the more people feel heard and appreciated, the more they will listen when it's your turn to talk.

One thing that has helped me talk to people of differing beliefs is setting up ground rules for spiritual discussions. I simply say, "Hey, I'm sure that we want this to be a good conversation and not turn into some kind of uncomfortable argument. So I'm going to let you share with me first everything you want to about what you believe. I'll ask you some questions along the way, if that's okay with you. My intent is not going to be to argue with you, but to understand where you are coming from. When you are completely finished sharing, then I'm going to ask you to allow me to share my beliefs with you so that you can completely understand me. Please feel free to ask me questions along the way. After that we can discuss, not argue about, areas we agree on and disagree on. Does that sound good to you?"

Every single time I begin a potentially volatile discussion with someone I've just recently met and I suggest these ground rules, they agree. The result? True communication as opposed to a showdown with my gospel gun!

2. Be slow to get angry.

The book of James also reminds us to be slow to anger. This can be especially difficult if you are sharing the gospel with somebody who wants to argue.

Refuse to get angry. Quietly call upon the Holy Spirit who is living inside you and ask God to give you the patience and love you need not to allow the conversation to turn into a cage match.

One of the things I deeply respect about many of the Mormon missionaries I have met is that they have been trained never to argue. They share verses from the Book of Mormon, quote from Mormon experts, and share their version of the gospel (different from ours, by the way), but they do so without hardly ever raising their voices.

We need to take a cue from The Church of Jesus Christ of Latter Day Saints in this area. The more we learn to refuse to argue and show love to others, the more effective at defending our faith we will be.

Go Figure!

Ask for God's help as you read Acts 8:26-40 and answer the following questions:

1. How did Philip start the conversation with the Ethiopian eunuch?

   _____

   _____

   _____

2. Did Philip use a threatening or nonthreatening question?

   _____

   _____

   _____

3. Why is this important?

   _____

   _____

   _____

4. Did he invite himself into the chariot or wait to be invited?

   _____

   _____

   _____

5. Why is this important?

_____

_____

_____

6. What does the phrase "then Philip began with that very passage" show us about how we are to share our faith with somebody from a different point of view?

_____

_____

_____

So What?

This chapter may have dramatically changed your perspective on how to defend your faith. The goal is not to out-debate or even win an argument. Defending your faith is not a win/lose scenario, it is a win/win scenario where if you listen and mutually respect others, you win by being able to share the gospel, and others win by hearing the gospel message! Remember, in many cases, people don't care what you know until they know that you care!

Let's leave guns to the hunters, soldiers, and police officers. When it comes to sharing the message of Jesus, leave your gospel gun and hate bullets at home. Instead, learn to ask questions, listen, love, and share the good news in the midst of a real conversation.

YOU'RE NEXT

It's been said that the best offense is a good defense. One of the best defenses for your belief system you can have is The 4-1 Defensive Formation, developed by my friends Bill Jack, who is with

The Worldview Academy, and Andrew Heister. The 4-1 Defense has four questions and one statement. Here's what it looks like:

4 questions

1. What do you mean by that?

This makes a person define the terms of his or her position.

2. How do you know that to be true?

This makes a person explain the logic/facts of his or her position.

3. What difference has it made in your life?

This makes a person defend the value of his or her position.

4. What if you are wrong?

This makes a person think the unthinkable about his or her position.

1 statement

1. I don't know, but I will find out.

This is the proper (and truthful!) response that we need to use when we don't have a good or knowledgeable answer. Many times we just try to make something up, but it is much better to admit our ignorance and promise to get back to them with an answer.

Take some time and go through each of the four questions and write out how you would answer them if they were asked of you about your faith. Here are some examples.

Q: What do you mean by salvation?

A: Salvation, according to the Bible, is what a person is given when he or she trusts in Christ as his or her only way to heaven. That person is saved from an eternity in hell.

Q: How do you know the Bible is true?

A: No other book in the world is so unique. It was written by 40 radically different men over the course of about 1,500 years on three different continents and yet has one theme and no contradictions. Also, it contains hundreds of prophecies that came true exactly as predicted!

_____

_____

_____

_____

_____

_____

_____

_____

* * *

For more info on **The Big Q: How do I defend my faith?** visit www.dare2share.org/soulfuel/archives and check out *Soul Fuel* question #27.

CHAPTER 29

"You Stinker!"

Fighting is stupid, childish, and immature. In other words it's something that a lot of high school guys do (or at the very minimum tell others around them they know how to do). I was no different as a teenager.

Maybe it's the mixture of watching girls, growing pains, and the introduction of testosterone into pubescent male bodies that causes it. Maybe it's just a guy thing. Maybe it is the way God made teenage boys. Whatever "it" is, it is reality with a lot of guys.

To be honest, I always got a kick out of watching two high school boys face off in a chest-to-chest prefight ritual. Have you ever noticed what takes place in those moments right before a fight goes down? For one, guys puff up like peacocks. They stick their chests out and stand flexed and ready. Add to this "crazy eyes" and you have a recipe for flying fists or at least a pushing match.

Quick side note: If you are a guy and reading this right now, let me give you a sure way of getting out of a fight. If another guy gets in your grill and is ready to throw fists when he asks, "Do you want to fight?" say in your best Spanish-accented voice, "No! I want to dance!" He will run. If he doesn't, you run.

Anyway, back to the point at hand. Right before "go time" guys usually try to say something that sounds tough. The tough-guy statements seem to be limited to things like this:

"Come on. Come on."

"Are you talking to me?"

"You don't want none of this."

"Go ahead and hit me." (This one always seemed a little weird to me.)

With such a limited array of tough-guy sayings, it's no wonder a lot of guys never actually get to the fight. Instead of a real fight it usually morphs into a glorified pushing match that is broken up quickly by those around them.

Have you ever seen a high school guy mess up a tough-guy statement right before a fight? It's not pretty. Believe me, I know.

Being raised in the toughest part of our city, I was no stranger to the fist-fighting brand of violence. When I started going to a Christian school in the suburbs, I thought most of the guys at our private school were kind of wimpy.

So when I went face-to-face and toe-to-toe with one of my friends (who was not a wimp, by the way) over a comment he said about my girlfriend, I was ready to throw down right away. We stood there facing each other, going through the checklist of the obligatory high school prefight ritual:

Standing up

Puffing our chests out (as much as they could be, anyway)

Getting crazy eyes

Saying something tough . . . or trying to, anyway.

His tough-guy saying went fine. It was a traditional, "I'm going to kick your rear." Standard at best . . . yet effective.

But I wanted something different, something unique, something shocking. But the only thing that came to my mind were two words: "You stink." And I even messed that one up. When these words spilled from my lips they came out, "YOU STINKER!"

Now let me tell you something: It's tough to sound tough when you use the word *stinker* in any context. You don't hear movie action heroes saying to the bad guys, "I'm going to defeat all of you stinkers!" Even comic book heroes wouldn't stoop to using this goofy insult against their evil nemeses.

Needless to say, there was no fight that day. My buddy was on the ground, howling in laughter as I stood in stooped humiliation, pondering what had just happened.

All this talk of fighting may kind of freak you out. You may be thinking, *Aren't we as Christians supposed to be peace-loving?* The answer is a great big YES with only one exception. We are to be in a constant battle with our three nemeses: the world, the flesh, and the devil. We are to wage war against the worldly system of temptation, our own tendencies to do wrong, and Satan and his army of demons. But for us to go chest-to-chest and eye-to-eye with such powerful forces, we need supernatural strength that can come only through the Holy Spirit. Only through borrowing God's strength as made available through His Spirit can we win against sin and Satan.

The Big Q: How do I get plugged in to the power of the Holy Spirit?

Remember not to think of the Holy Spirit as a vague, impersonal force, but as a distinct person of the Trinity who has tremendous power and strength. It was through the power of the Holy Spirit that Jesus did His miracles (Hebrews 2:3-5) and even rose from the dead (Romans 1:4). The Holy Spirit was involved in the creation of the universe (Genesis 1:1-2); is actively involved in convicting the world of sin, righteousness, and judgment (John 16:8-11); and will be involved in the final judgment of the world (Revelation 2:7).

Make no mistake about it, the power of the Holy Spirit is immeasurable and amazing. What makes it so amazing is that He makes His power available to you and to me.

Take a long look at this verse, "Do not get drunk on wine, which leads to debauchery. Instead, be filled with the Spirit" (Ephesians 5:18).

Through this passage God is telling us that when we are filled with wine, we are controlled by the alcohol in that wine. When we are filled with the Spirit, we are controlled by God.

When we are filled with or controlled by the Spirit, His power shows itself in all sorts of relevant ways. For one, we produce what the Bible has nicknamed "the fruit of the Spirit."

BLAST FROM THE PAST

The average Christian is so cold and contented with his wretched condition that there is no vacuum of desire into which the blessed Spirit can rush in satisfying fullness.[1]

—A. W. Tozer, 20th century pastor

Galatians 5:22-23 tells us what that fruit is: "But the fruit of the Spirit is love, joy, peace, patience, kindness, goodness, faithfulness, gentleness and self-control."

Basically, these verses remind us that if we are controlled by the power of the Spirit, instead of being puffed up and full of proud posturing, we will be loving, patient, and so on with everyone we encounter. Our life will be marked not by strife, backstabbing, or hate. Instead we will be branded with a selflessness that can only come from the Spirit of God.

Calling this "the fruit of the Spirit" is a great analogy. If you're like me, when you hear that phrase you probably imagine a tree packed full of all sorts of oranges or apples. In a spiritual sense, we are like trees that have our roots in God's Word. The Spirit of God is like the nutritious sap that flows through our branches so that the fruit is produced. What's the bottom line? No sap, no fruit!

Outside of the Spirit of God we don't have the power to truly forgive or to overcome lust, pride, or anger. It is only through His strength that we can live like Jesus.

If we are operating in His power, then we have victory over Satan and sin. We live victorious lives that make God smile and bring us true and lasting joy.

If we are not, then we are toast.

Go Figure!

Open your Bible and read John 14:26-27.

1. Why does Jesus call the Holy Spirit the Counselor?

_____

_____

_____

2. What teachings of Jesus will the Holy Spirit remind us of?

_____

_____

_____

3. What does being filled with the Spirit have to do with having peace?

_____

_____

_____

4. How can the Holy Spirit help your heart not be troubled?

_____

_____

_____

5. How could being filled with the Spirit help you not be afraid?

_____

_____

_____

6. Are you willing to let the Holy Spirit fill you every day? Why or why not?

_____

_____

_____

So how does a person plug in to the power of the Spirit? Do we have to say some magic prayer? Do we have to conjure Him up in some kind of spiritual voodoo ritual? Do we have to sing worship songs so loudly and intensely that God finally releases the power of His Spirit?

No! It's much simpler than that. All we must do is yield ourselves to Him. Basically, that means that by choice we give the steering wheel of our lives to God. We consciously submit ourselves fully to His control.

If you want to express this choice to yield to God you could pray something like, "God, I submit myself fully to You. I confess my sins to You right now, recognizing my utter dependence on Your Spirit to live in victory over those sins. Take control of me fully by

Your Spirit and give me the desire and strength to live by Your power today."

As you recognize your sins before God and choose to forsake them, you are opening the channel of communication to God through prayer. Through this open channel the power of the Spirit can flow through you.

Now you may not "feel" any different after you've asked the Spirit to take control of you, but feelings have nothing to do with it. This is a matter of faith, not feeling. You are choosing to walk in utter dependence on God moment by moment that day.

Take it from me, there will be times you have to get back into what I call "The Power Zone." When we choose to sin instead of submitting, we cut off the power supply of the Spirit, but when we confess that sin and yield to the Spirit again, He takes over the steering wheel to our lives. If you are like me, then there is a consistent battle to see who is going to "drive" my day, the Spirit of God or me.

All of us have heard of the Declaration of Independence. This manuscript, penned by Thomas Jefferson, declared to the King of England that the colonies of America were now the United States of America, an independent country. On July 4, 1776, we officially broke from England and became our own nation.

 INSANE BRAIN STRAIN
How can you tell if the Spirit of God is controlling you or if you are controlling yourself?

What every Christian teen needs is his or her very own Declaration of *Dependence*. Instead of breaking off from the King of the universe and trying to run our own lives, we are signing, so to speak, a daily declaration of dependence on the Spirit of God. Although you may think of dependence as a sign of weakness, it is when we are weak that we are truly strong.

So What?

Choose to live a life of utter dependence on God. Ask Him every day to give you the strength. He will give you all the power you need to live in victory over sin, Satan, and all the stuff that stands in your way.

When you are living in a daily declaration of dependence on God, the fruit of the Spirit will permeate your life and your relationships. You will discover the joy, power, and life-altering impact of being filled with the Spirit.

YOU'RE NEXT!

Write out your own Declaration of Dependence to God, listing the things you want to give over to Him and areas you need help with. For example:

Dear God,

Today on this date _____, I solemnly declare my complete dependence on You. I turn over control of _____ (where I go when I surf the Internet, what I say when I talk with my friends . . . you fill in the blank with whatever God is challenging you to give over to Him) and I ask for Your power to overcome the bad attitudes I have in my life. I thank You that the Holy Spirit loves me and fills me when I turn my life over to Him.

_____

_____

_____

_____

_____

_____

_____

_____

_____

_____

_____

_____

* * *

For more info on The Big Q: **How do I get plugged in to the power of the Holy Spirit?** visit www.dare2share.org/soulfuel/archives and check out *Soul Fuel* question #7.

CHAPTER 30

Choose to Lose

During my teen years, I wasn't a Lone Ranger Christian. I had a circle of friends who were full-on fanatics for Jesus.

I met Art when I was 11 years old. He dedicated his life to Jesus Christ and, as I shared in chapter 21, he gave his all to share the gospel with anyone and everyone who would listen. What did Art end up doing with his life? . . .

At first I thought Rick was a cocky little seventh-grader who needed taking down a notch or two. But the more I got to know him the more I realized he was a junior-high-school kid who loved Jesus more than anything and anyone. Being the jock that he was, he played basketball with a fury and an intensity that you rarely see on any court. In one game in high school he scored 60 points. I actually taught Rick to play basketball, and he beat me three hours later (that shouldn't surprise you). But it didn't really bother me. Rick was my friend, and he brought the same intensity he showed in sports to his relationship with Jesus. What is Rick doing now? . . .

Scott may be the funniest, smartest, and most witty guy I have ever met. We rode the same school bus at Arvada Christian School and became good friends in our teen years. We used to make homemade movies with his parents' camcorder and spend countless hours watching and analyzing movies. On weekends I would stay at his house and watch movies until early in the morning. But Scott loved Jesus even more than he loved movies. Although he had a lot of questions about what it means to be a servant of God in a dazed and confused world, he kept pursuing his relationship with God. Can you guess what Scott is doing now? . . .

We were all committed to the Lord Jesus, but each of us has learned to express that in different ways and very different professions. Art, Rick, and Scott were my friends in high school and remain my friends to this day. Although each of us took a different path in life, we all have chosen to live a life for God in our own unique ways.

Art became a truck driver. Everywhere he goes, he shares the good news of Jesus with as many people as he can. More than 20 years after high school, he still faithfully preaches the gospel wherever he goes and to whomever he meets. His goal is to be the best truck driver he can be so that he can bring honor and glory to the God he loves so much.

Rick became a pastor of a large and growing church. He takes the same intensity he had on the basketball court to plying the pulpit at his church (which happens to be my church, too). Every week when I go to church and hear his sermons, I still remember him as a force of nature on the basketball court and in his service to God. Today he also helps coach a Christian high school basketball team. It encourages me to see how many teens he has impacted with his passion for Jesus.

As for Scott? He is directing major Hollywood films. His goal is to write and direct movies that jolt people into thinking about God. But, being the madman for God that he is, he has decided to do much of that through the supernatural/thriller genre. In the fall of 2005 Sony Pictures released *The Exorcism of Emily Rose*. The movie received rave reviews by both secular and Christian critics. I remember sitting in a prescreening of the movie with hundreds of people, many of them teenagers, as the movie began. I was there with Bob Waliszewski, the editor of *Plugged In* and one of the movie reviewers for Focus on the Family. Both Bob and I were impacted and encouraged by Scott's vision and the quality of the movie. For two hours, Scott took us on an unbelievable journey that made everybody in the audience take a second look at God.

Scott Derrickson has experienced major success in Hollywood and, I believe, is well on his way to being a household name. Scott is, by far, the most talented guy I have ever met. But the reason I respect him so much is because, in spite of the temptations that surround him, he is committed first and foremost to Jesus.

Ultimately, what makes you a sold-out servant of Jesus? The answer may surprise you. It's worship.

When you choose to lose yourself so that you can serve God with all your heart, soul, mind, and might, it doesn't matter what others think. It doesn't matter if you are good at basketball, driving trucks, preaching, or directing movies. The point is that in everything you do, you worship God.

The Big Q: How can I really worship God in everything I do?

When you think of the word *worship* you may think of singing songs at your church or listening to a worship CD in your car or room. But the concept behind the word *worship* goes way beyond just music.

The idea of worship is to give glory, honor, and praise to God. It basically means that we are choosing to exalt and elevate Him in our words, thoughts, and actions. Singing worship songs is just one form of worship.

So how else can you worship God?

You can worship God by the way you work, study, play sports, share your faith, or eat a cheeseburger. That's right. Paul writes in 1 Corinthians 10:31, "So whether you eat or drink or whatever you do, do it all for the glory of God." Everything we do is either for the glory of God or out of selfish motives. There is no in between—and when we do things for the glory of God . . . that's worship!

> **BLAST FROM THE PAST**
>
> The Christian faith is meant to be lived moment by moment. It isn't some broad, general outline—it's a long walk with a real Person. Details count: passing thoughts, small sacrifices, a few encouraging words, little acts of kindness, brief victories over nagging sins.[1]
>
> —JONI EARECKSON TADA, 20TH CENTURY ARTIST

The Worship Test

I want you to take this worship test. The goal is to see how well you worship God in your life. Be honest as you take this three-part test (kind of important if you are taking a test on worship!).

Part #1 Write down the top five priorities in your life, ranking them in the order of their importance. Let me give you an example. When I first took this test, my five priorities went something like:

Spending time with God

Spending time with my family

Doing well at school

Working hard at my job

Hanging out with my friends

So what are your five top priorities in order of their importance? Be honest!

1. _____
2. _____
3. _____
4. _____
5. _____

Part #2 Write down how much time you spend on each of these priorities during an average day. For instance, how much time did you spend with God, family, at school, with friends, etc.? This is where the honesty part kicks in.

Part #3 Reorder your priorities with what you spend the most time doing at the top and the least time doing at the bottom. List them below.

1. _____
2. _____
3. _____
4. _____
5. _____

Did your first list radically differ from your last list? When I first took this test, mine did. Spending time with God ended up as number five and doing well at school was number one.

I remember the pangs of conscience I had when I first took this test. I felt I had somehow missed the mark as a Christian. Are you experiencing any of the same uneasy feelings I did when I took this test?

 INSANE BRAIN STRAIN

How is it possible for sinful, mortal people to bring glory to a holy and infinite God?

The guy who gave me this test then surprised me with a statement that went something like, "If you are feeling guilty as you

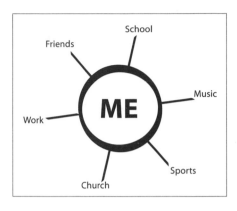

look at how much your list has changed, it's because you have bought a lie. The list is the lie."

At first I had no idea what he was talking about until he drew two circles on a chalkboard. The first circle had the word "Me" in the middle of it. Extending out from the circle were all sorts of little spokes with words like "work," "school," "friends," "hobbies," "church," and "God" on them.

He went on to tell me something like, "You see, when you are in the center of your life, then everything from sports to family to job

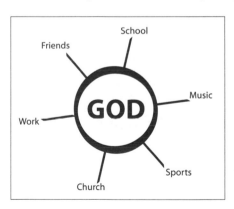

to, yes, even God, is just a spoke extending out from the most important thing to you in your world . . . you." My friend then drew another circle with something different in the middle.

What he shared next changed my perspective forever. "When God is in the center of the circle of your life, then everything extending out is an expression of worship of Him. Whether it be work or sports or friends or whatever, everything you do should extend out of your love for God. Then your life is a living, breathing act of ongoing worship."

His words rattled my life. He then went on to say the test he gave was a farce. Our tendency to make priority lists with God at the top is a sham, because God *is* the list. When He is at the center of our circle, so to speak, then everything we do erupts from our relationship with Him. This is in agreement with the verse, "So whether you eat or drink or whatever you do, do it all for the glory of God" (1 Corinthians 10:31).

Go Figure!

Open your Bible and read 1 Corinthians 6:19-20. Ask for God's insight as you answer these questions:

1. What words would you use to describe how you feel knowing that your body is actually the temple of the Holy Spirit?

    _____

    _____

    _____

2. Does knowing that the Holy Spirit lives inside you motivate you to worship God?

    _____

    _____

    _____

3. If you are "not your own," who does "own" you?

    _____

    _____

    _____

4. Who "bought" you?

_____

_____

_____

5. What was the price He paid for you?

_____

_____

_____

6. How does knowing God owns you impact your view of worship?

_____

_____

_____

7. What are some specific ways you can honor God, not only with your body, but with your heart, soul, mind, and might?

_____

_____

_____

So What?

In a very practical sense this means we should bring the circle of God's presence into every area of our lives. Teens tend to separate "God stuff" and "their stuff." Many seem to think that God stuff includes things like going to youth group, having a daily time with God in His Word, going to camps and retreats, and such. Their stuff is pretty much everything else, like whom they date, where they go on the Internet, what they wear, what kind of music they listen to, what sports they play, whom they hang with as friends, how they approach homework, and so on.

The change of thinking I'm asking you to make is to realize that it is *all* God stuff. He wants to be the Master of everything in your life. But He will not force His way in. Being the gentleman that He is, He has left it up to you to take the initiative.

How do you begin to do that? You start by making one big decision to let Him rule in the center of the circle of your life. I believe that's what Romans 12:1 is getting at when it powerfully reminds us, "Therefore, I urge you, brothers, in view of God's mercy, to offer your bodies as living sacrifices, holy and pleasing to God—this is your spiritual act of worship."

How do you worship God in everything you do? You offer yourself as a living sacrifice! The Old Testament tells us that Jews sacrificed (killed) certain kinds of animals all the time as an act of worship. Lambs, bulls, and goats cost money, so sacrificing one showed that the Jews were making a financial sacrifice to worship God. The blood that was shed pointed ahead to the death of Jesus, the ultimate sin sacrifice.

But in this life-rattling verse, God is calling us to offer our bodies as "living sacrifices." In other words, we are to die without dying. We are to die to our own selfish desires and choose to live, letting God rule the center circle of our lives.

Are there times we push God out of the circle? Yes! But as soon as we realize it, we back down and let Him rule again.

The verse calls this process "your spiritual act of worship." In other words, allowing God to call the shots in your life is your ultimate act of bringing honor to God. Your life becomes a worship song, and everything you do, say, and think rises like a song of praise to the heavens.

Art is singing that song by driving trucks.

Rick is singing that song by preaching sermons.

Scott is singing that song by directing movies.

I am singing that song by leading Dare 2 Share Ministries.

And it's not what we do for a living that is an act of worship. It's everything we do from the time we get up to the time we go to sleep.

One of the biggest reasons I'm seeking to be a living sacrifice for God today is because of the friends I had throughout my junior high and high school years. I thank God for Art, Rick, and Scott, this coalition of friends and Jesus freaks! We challenged each other to serve God and Him alone, no matter what, no matter how crazy others thought we were.

By the way, do you have some sold-out servants of Jesus around you? If you truly want to be a Jesus worshiper, a song of praise to God, a living sacrifice, you need a tribe of Jesus freaks to surround you who will encourage you while pushing you to the brink of spiritual intensity.

What will be the result of life with God at the center, with friends who are doing the same? People will think you are nuts. They will ask why you won't go to that party or just try a drink, smoke, toke, or whatever. They will make fun of you for being a prude or rude for not accepting their offer. They will wonder why you won't go to certain movies with them or jam to the same music or hang at the same clubs. They will scratch their heads when you don't laugh at the same jokes or visit the same sites. They may think you are crazy. But take heart. We come from a long line of "lunatics."

I've spent this whole book telling stories of how God used His holy Word and the incidents from my early years to teach me about Himself and give me a passion to serve Him with all of my heart. Now its your turn. But be warned: This kind of commitment comes with a price tag. You will be mocked by some of your friends and whispered about by others. Some will think you have gone crazy.

Just remember the words of Jesus in Matthew 5:11-12, "Blessed are you when people insult you, persecute you and falsely say all kinds of evil against you because of me. Rejoice and be glad, because great is your reward in heaven, for in the same way they persecuted the prophets who were before you."

At our Dare 2 Share conferences we hold across the nation, we equip thousands of teens to share their faith. We have instituted a tradition at these conferences we call "PU," which stands for Persecution University. When a teen comes to Dare 2 Share, gets trained to share his or her faith, is turned loose to collect canned food and share Jesus, and then that teen has the door slammed in his or her face, then that teen has graduated from "PU." If these students share their testimony on the Saturday night, they get a standing ovation from the thousands upon thousands of teenagers in the crowd.

The same thing happens every day when you choose to live a life worthy of God. When you know, live, and share your faith every single day, and when you inevitably get slammed for it, I believe there are crowds—not of thousands, but millions of angels and saints—looking over the banister of heaven, giving you a standing O. Picture that the next time you are discouraged because a friend shut you down when you started sharing the gospel with him or her.

As I wrap up this book, I want to thank you for making it through this rather long manuscript. I hope you enjoyed reading it half as much as I enjoyed writing it. I'm a storyteller by nature and love to articulate in vivid terms the incidents, accidents, and plain old dents that happened to me along the way in my crazy life.

But *You're Next* is not simply about me and my story. This book is a theology book that tackles the 30 tough questions at the core of Christianity. But, ultimately, this is not just a theology book.

My goal in writing *You're Next* was for *you* to be next. My prayer is that you will have a collision with the God of the Bible and these

30 core truths in your life. My hope is that you allow the Trinity to impact the way you view MySpace, that you let the truth of God's Word transform your relationships, and that you allow the reality of judgment day to impact the way you study in school. Ultimately, my prayer is that every single one of the 30 core truths in this book impacts every area of your life in a real and powerful way.

In other words, the reason that I wrote this book about God, theology, and me is so that you will allow God to write the story of your life using the truth of His Word as the ink that permanently marks every area of your life.

You're next!

YOU'RE NEXT!

It's your turn to let God write the story of your life with His truth. Think of one story from your life and what it taught you about God. Write it out as if you were beginning to write the story of your own life.

_____

_____

_____

_____

_____

_____

_____

_____

✳ ✳ ✳

For more info on **The Big Q: How can I really worship God in everything I do?** visit www.dare2share.org/soulfuel/archives and check out *Soul Fuel* question #30.

The Big Q Chart

Each of the 30 chapters in this book deals with a key question and core truth of Christianity. You can explore these core truths further by signing up to receive *Soul Fuel,* a free weekly e-mail blast. Every week *Soul Fuel* specifically addresses one of these 30 key questions. Free weekly *Soul Fuel* Youth Leader Guides and Parent/Teen Discussion Guides are also available. To sign up for *Soul Fuel* or to access it online, at www.dare2share.org/soulfuel.

Dare 2 Share youth conferences, held in numerous cities across the nation, equip and motivate thousands of teens each year to know, live, share, and own their faith in Jesus. Each year's conference tour is designed around a specific selection of the 30 questions, with all 30 questions addressed in the course of a five-year conference cycle. For more information on a Dare 2 Share conference near you, visit www.dare2share.org/conference.

The 30 Big Q's

Chapter 1   Who is God, and what is He like?

Chapter 2   Who am I, where did I come from, and what is my purpose?

Chapter 3   What is sin, and how does it impact my life and my relationship with others?

Chapter 4   Why does God allow evil in this world?

Chapter 5   Who are Satan and his demons?

Chapter 6   Who is Jesus?

Chapter 7   Is there a real heaven and hell, and what are they like?

Chapter 8   How do I know Jesus really rose from the dead?

Chapter 9   What is a Christian, and how does a person become one?

Chapter 10   Is the Bible really God's Word, and does it really relate to my life?

Chapter 11   What is prayer, and how do I do it?

Chapter 12   Did God create everything, and why does it matter?

Chapter 13   Will God ever leave or forsake me?

Chapter 14   What is the church, and why should I be involved?

Chapter 15   Why should I study the Bible, and how do I do it?

Chapter 16   Is there a judgment day, and what difference should it make in my life?

Chapter 17   How should the return of Christ impact my life?

Chapter 18   What are spiritual gifts, and how do I discover mine?

Chapter 19   How do I engage in spiritual warfare?

Chapter 20   What is the Great Commission, and how does it relate to me?

Chapter 21   What about people who have never heard the gospel?

Chapter 22   What is truth, and can I know it with certainty?

Chapter 23   Who is the Holy Spirit, and what does He do?

Chapter 24   Can I really be forgiven for all my sins, even the really bad ones?

Chapter 25   Why did Jesus die on the cross?

Chapter 26   If Jesus is the only way to heaven, are all other religions wrong?

Chapter 27   What is the Trinity?

Chapter 28   How do I defend my faith?

Chapter 29   How do I get plugged in to the power of the Holy Spirit?

Chapter 30   How can I really worship God in everything I do?

Notes

Chapter 1

1. *Creeds of Christendom*, "The Nicene Creed," http://www.creeds.net/ancient/nicene.htm.

Chapter 2

1. CRTA, "Historic Church Documents," Westminster Shorter Catechism, http://www.reformed.org/documents/wsc/index.html.

Chapter 3

1. Think Exist, "Thinkexist.com," *John Calvin Quotes*, http://think exist.com/quotation/though_satan_instills_his_poison-and_fans_the/170620.html.

Chapter 4

1. OrthodoxyToday.org, John Kapsalis, "When Bad Things Aren't Supposed to Happen," http://www.orthodoxytoday.org/articles6/Kapsalis Hope.php.

Chapter 5

1. The Gospel Truth, GospelTruth.net, People God Has Used, William Booth and Catherine Booth, Written Works, Catherine Booth, *Life and Death*, "Religious Indifference," http://www.gospeltruth.net/booth/cath_booth/life_and_death/cbooth_1_indifference.htm.

Chapter 6

1. C. S. Lewis, *Mere Christianity* (New York: Simon & Schuster, 1996), page 56.

Chapter 7

1. Adapted from Greg Stier, *Dare 2 Share* (Carol Stream, Ill.: Focus on the Family Tyndale House Publishers, Inc., 2006), pages 14-15.
2. HePrayed.com, Quotes, William Booth, http://www.heprayed.com/ quotes.asp?filterAuthor=William+Booth&filterSubject=All&filter Order=rating+desc.

Chapter 8

1. Go to the Bible.Com, *Dwight L. Moody Sermons,* "Shall We Meet Our Loved Ones Again?" http://www.gotothebible.com/HTML/Sermons/ lovedones.html.
2. Dr. Andrea Berlin and Dr. Jodi Magness, "Two Archaeologists Comment on The Passion of the Christ," Archaeological Institute of America, March 2004, http://www.archaeological.org/pdfs/papers/Comments_ on_The_Passion.pdf.
3. Dr. John Ankerberg and Dr. John Weldon, Ankerberg Theological Research Institute, "Does the Evidence For the Resurrection Offer Proof that Jesus Rose From the Dead?" http://www.ankerberg.com/ Articles/editors-choice/EC0403W2.htm.
4. World Net Daily, Hal Lindsay, "Is He Risen?" http://www.wnd.com/ news/article.asp?ARTICLE_ID=22374.
5. Leadership U, Josh McDowell, "Evidence for the Resurrection," http://www.leaderu.com/everystudent/easter/articles/josh2.html.

Chapter 9

1. John Newton, "Amazing Grace," *Hymns for the Living Church* (Carol Stream, Ill.: Hope Publishing Company, 1982), page 288.

Chapter 10

1. Translated by Benedicta Ward, *The Sayings of the Desert Fathers* (Kalamazoo, Mich.: Cistercian Publications Inc., 1984), page 192.

2. BrainyMedia.com, "Brainy Quote," *Josh McDowell Quotes*, http://www.brainyquote.com/quotes/authors/j/josh_mcdowell.html.

3. Josh McDowell, *The New Evidence that Demands a Verdict* (Nashville: Thomas Nelson, 1999), page 193.

Chapter 11

1. Tentmaker, Wisdom Quotes, Prayer Quotes, Brother Lawrence, http://www.tentmaker.org/Quotes/prayerquotes.htm.

Chapter 12

1. Christian Truth and Its Defense, Weekly Quotes Archive, Dr. Duane T. Gish, http://www.christiantruthanditsdefense.org/quotesarchive.

Chapter 13

1. ChristianityToday.com, Reflections: Mercy, Augustine, *The Confessions.* http://www.christianitytoday.com/ct/2003/005/29.60.html.

Chapter 14

1. BrainyMedia.com, "Brainy Quote," *George Fox Quotes*, http://www.brainyquote.com/quotes/quotes/g/georgefox182499.html.

Chapter 15

1. Mark Galli and Ted Olsen, *131 Christians Everyone Should Know* (Nashville, Tenn.: Broadman & Holman Publishers, 2000), page 337.

Chapter 16

1. Christdesert.org. Benedictine Holy Rule, Chapter 4, verse 47, http://www.christdesert.org/noframes/holyrule/chapter4.46-78.html.

Chapter 17

1. Faith Bible Baptist Church, "One Step at a Time Christian Growth Series," *Step 41 – The Last Days,* http://www.fbbc.com/messages/one_step/one_step_41.htm.

2. Think Exist, "Thinkexist.com," *Theodore Epp Quotes*, http://en.think exist.com/quotation/live-as-though-christ-died-yesterday-rose-from/ 1084732.html.

Chapter 18

1. BrainyMedia.com, "Brainy Quote," *Mother Teresa Quotes*, http://www .brainyquote.com/quotes/authors/m/mother_teresa.html.

Chapter 19

1. World of Quotes.com, *Ignatius Loyola Quotes*, http://www.world ofquotes.com/author/Ignatius-Loyola/1/index.html.

Chapter 20

1. Sermon Illustrator, *Evangelism Quotes and Illustrations*, C. T. Studd, 14, http://www.sermonillustrator.org/minisermons/folder2/evangelism% 20quotes%20and%20illustrations.htm.

Chapter 21

1. Oswald Chambers, *My Utmost for His Highest* (Grand Rapids, Mich.: Discovery House Publishers, 1992), October 14.

Chapter 22

1. Wholesomewords.org, *Quotes & Notes*, No. 18, Matthew Henry, http://www.wholesomewords.org/devotion3.html.

Chapter 23

1. HymnSite.com, Charles Wesley, Jesus, Thine All-Victorious Love, http://www.hymnsite.com/lyrics/umh422.sht.

Chapter 24

1. Think Exist, "Thinkexist.com," *John Bunyan Quotes*, http://en.think exist.com/quotes/john_bunyan.

Chapter 25

1. Tentmaker, Wisdom Quotes, "The Cross/Identifying with Christ, Martin Luther," http://www.tentmaker.org/Quotes/thecrossquotes.htm.

Chapter 26

1. Christian Apologetics & Research Ministry, Creeds, *Augsburg Confession,* Article VI. http://www.carm.org/creeds/augsburg.htm#augs-004.

Chapter 27

1. Christian Classics Ethereal Library, Spurgeon's Sermons Volume 6: 1860, Sermon 291. *A Christmas Question,* http://www.ccel.org/ccel/spurgeon/sermons06.vi.html?highlight=gnat seek to drink in the ocean - highlight.

Chapter 28

1. The Tertullian Project, Wit and Wisdom, Quotations, http://www.tertullian.org/quotes.htm.

Chapter 29

1. The Quotable Christian, Christians, A. W. Tozer, http://www.pietyhilldesign.com/gcq/quotepages/zeal.html.

Chapter 30

1. Tentmaker, Wisdom Quotes, Keys to Christian Living Quotes, http://www.tentmaker.org/Quotes/keys.htm.

About the Author

Greg Stier is the founder and president of Dare 2 Share Ministries (D2S). Greg lives in Arvada, Colorado, with his wife, Debbie, and children, Jeremy and Kailey. Over the last decade, Greg has impacted the lives of hundreds of thousands of teenagers across the country through Dare 2 Share training conferences. Dare 2 Share's vision is to train one million Christian teens across the nation to transform their world. To learn more, check out Greg's blog at www.gregstier.org. Greg's prayer is that God will use the ministry and these training conferences to launch a spiritual awakening through an army of youth leaders, teenagers, pastors, and parents.

D2S also provides free online resources and a vast array of curriculum, books, and other training resources for students and youth leaders. For more information on Dare 2 Share training conferences or how to start an e-team (a team of students who lead the way for outreach) go to www.dare2share.org. Look for the free resource *Soul Fuel* and sign up to receive it online.

Dare 2 Share Ministries

dare2share.org

(800) 462-8355

PO Box 745323

Arvada, CO 80006-5323

www.gregstier.org

FOCUS ON THE FAMILY®

teen outreach

At Focus on the Family, we work to help you really get to know Jesus and equip you to change your world for Him.

We realize the struggles you face are different from your parents' or your little brother's, so we've developed a lot of resources specifically to help you live boldly for Christ, no matter what's happening in your life.

Besides teen events and a live call-in show, we have Web sites, magazines, booklets, devotionals and novels ... all dealing with the stuff you care about. For a detailed listing of the latest resources, log on to our Web site at **go.family.org/teens**.

***Breakaway*®**
Teen guys
breakawaymag.com

Focus on the Family Magazines

We know you want to stay up-to-date on the latest in your world — but it's hard to find information on relationships, entertainment, trends and teen issues that doesn't drag you down. It's even harder to find magazines that deliver what you want and need from a Christ-honoring perspective.

That's why we created *Breakaway* (for teen guys), *Brio* (for teen girls 12 to 16), *Brio & Beyond* (for girls ages 16 and up). So, don't be left out — sign up today!

***Brio*®**
Teen girls 13 to 15
briomag.com

***Brio & Beyond*®**
Teen girls 16 to 19
briomag.com

Phone toll free: (800) A-FAMILY (232-6459)
In Canada, call toll free: (800) 661-9800

BP06XTN